BUDDHISM

The Complete Guide to Buddhism and Meditation
to Relieve Stress

(A Personal Exploration of Buddhism in Today's World)

Brooks Herring

Published by Andrew Zen

Brooks Herring

All Rights Reserved

Buddhism: The Complete Guide to Buddhism and Meditation to Relieve Stress (A Personal Exploration of Buddhism in Today's World)

ISBN 978-1-77485-197-5

All rights reserved. No part of this guide may be reproduced in any form without permission in writing from the publisher except in the case of brief quotations embodied in critical articles or reviews.

Legal & Disclaimer

The information contained in this book is not designed to replace or take the place of any form of medicine or professional medical advice. The information in this book has been provided for educational and entertainment purposes only.

The information contained in this book has been compiled from sources deemed reliable, and it is accurate to the best of the Author's knowledge; however, the Author cannot guarantee its accuracy and validity and cannot be held liable for any errors or omissions. Changes are periodically made to this book. You must consult your doctor or get professional medical advice before using any of the suggested remedies, techniques, or information in this book.

Upon using the information contained in this book, you agree to hold harmless the Author from and against any damages, costs, and expenses, including any legal fees potentially resulting from the application of any of the information provided by this guide. This disclaimer applies to any damages or injury caused by the use and application, whether directly or indirectly, of any advice or information presented, whether for breach of contract, tort, negligence, personal injury, criminal intent, or under any other cause of action.

You agree to accept all risks of using the information presented inside this book. You need to consult a professional medical practitioner in order to ensure you are both able and healthy enough to participate in this program.

Table of Contents

Introduction 1

Chapter 1: What Is Buddhism? 2

Chapter 2: The Teaching Of Buddhism 11

Chapter 3: How To Have The Right Thought, Right Speech And Right Understanding..............................27

Chapter 4: The Four Noble Truths..............................36

Chapter 5: Clearing The Path To Enlightenment........41

Chapter 6: The Mind Of A Buddhist 53

Chapter 7: The Eight-Fold Path 59

Chapter 8: Different Schools Of Buddhism 74

Chapter 9: Who Was Buddha?...................................79

Chapter 10: "Holding On To Anger Is Like Drinking Poison And Expecting The Other Person To Die." - Buddha...87

Chapter 11: Learning To Be Humble........................101

Chapter 12: In Depth Understanding Of Buddhism In Accordance To Daily Life..108

Chapter 13: Practicing The Teachings 112

Chapter 14: A New Way Of Seeing Yourself And The World..119

Chapter 15: Breaking Down Buddhism....................132

Chapter 16: The Circumstances For The Potentials For Happiness To Ripen 181

Chapter 17: How To Meditate 193

Conclusion..204

Introduction

We live in a stressful world which makes us wish we had a simpler life. In reality, there is no need to go back and rewind into the past to attain that blissful state that we all seek All we need to do is follow the path of spirituality and discover peace inside us in the midst of the chaos around us.

In this book, you'll discover how you can accomplish this, through the principles from the great and enlightened master that is the Buddha in a time of less than an entire week. It's true, in an hour or so we'll find ourselves on the correct path in achieving an unbridled peace we all deserve. Learn the most basic methods that can be followed by everyone, to live a lifestyle that is awash with the virtues that just lead to an unrestrained joy. All of this will be done within less than seven days!

Chapter 1: What Is Buddhism?

"A mind unperturbed by the vagaries of fortune, from sorrow freed, from defilements cleansed, from fear liberated -- this is the greatest blessing." -- The Buddha

Hi! You're probably the type of person who's eager to keep learning new things regularly. In all honesty is there any other reason to choose this book? It is a good idea to be interested in Buddhism.

You may have heard about it through a different source like online social networks or an acquaintance who is passionate in its lessons. You may also have learned about the many ways that it has assisted people who discover their purpose for existence, or to some extent - experience peace and calm in the seemingly fast-paced and stressful world. Many questions may be floating through your head regarding

Buddhism. Over time they will be answered.

In the beginning take a deep breath since you are here today: reading this book and acquiring the knowledge that will enable you to find true happiness everyday life. Take a look around and observe the way your body is making you feel alive. Your lungs continue to breathe and without you instructing it to do the case may be.

Your eyes naturally squint in order in order to ensure your eyes stay moist and secure. Your blood flows under your skin, largely not paying attention to your surroundings and other considerations. In addition, think about how you can take in the information on this page.

Do you think that this is not something to be grateful for? Give yourself a few minutes to think about this thought. Are you sure that you're still in this place?

It is a good idea, but for we are now able to answer what could be the primary inquiry in your mind Is there a Buddhism? What is Buddhism? Do you be aware that Buddhism is not a religious system?

In any case it is not in the sense that it is an organisation that outlines how one should to feel confident about an enthralling power. There isn't any divinity to worship regardless of the fact that one could be wondering why certain people seem to be adoring the statues of Buddha. Although there are those who worship his image (and incorrectly) however, true Buddhists just pay attention to the memories of Buddha.

They do not love or appeal to him. Many people who rise each day with the intention of practicing Buddhist lessons find motivation in the intricate image that depicts the Buddha.

It's similar to finding your source of inspiration in the actions of an efficient person. Buddhism is a philosophy that enables you to see the truth of the real world. The lessons are focused on developing your capacity to become aware of choices as well as your activities and the environment.

All of these lead the body to be connected to nature and your true self. The actions of Buddhism which include contemplation as well as yoga - are designed to help you overcome your beliefs about your self and the world around you.

They act as a guide to hold on to the qualities of respect, love, genuine discernment and mindfulness. People who follow the path of Buddhism typically achieve the state that is "flawless illumination."

At the conclusion of the day they transform into the form of a "Buddha." A Buddha is an individual who is able to comprehend the nature of life as it could be. The edified person then goes going with the flow, while and at the same time, observing the rules that is in line to this perspective. However, there is a lot of fascination in this regard, due to the fact that when you follow the practice of Buddhism there isn't an "true objective."

It's a conundrum for one to say that they are going to practice Buddhism with a particular end of achieving an edification. Who is The Buddha? "Buddha" means "the illuminated one" or "the stirred being."

It refers to any person who has achieved this state. In any case you might be able in thinking about the first Buddha. According to tradition, the primary Buddha was called Siddhartha Gautama. Many believe that he was created at the time of 563 B.C. in the land now located in Nepal.

It is believed that the Buddha was born to be an imperial, but at the age of 29 the Buddha realized no influence or luck gave him a real sense of satisfaction.

In this regard, what did he do was determined to research the same variety of religions around the world to find the answer to the question we are asked "Where would one be able to discover bliss?" After a few years of his spiritual journey and after a long time, the Buddha discovered "The Middle Path" while contemplating beneath the Bodhi tree.

The insights he received led him to achieve the perfect state of education. After the edification he received The Buddha was able to experience what is left of his life by sharing the knowledge he had gathered. The people who devoted themselves to the Buddha's teachings call his teachings the Dharma which means "Truth."

In the present, Buddhism is progressively turning into a popular lifestyle choice for large numbers of people across the globe. In fact, even people in the Western countries are pursuing the path of The Middle Path since they realize that it is a way to connect with their soul.

Another reason for the reason Buddhism is so widespread is that the Buddha was never a guarantee that he was a god. He was a rather an educator who imparted his wisdom based on his own insights and experiences in his life.

Furthermore the belief system of Buddhism can be described by some as "huge disapproved." This means that the people who practice it have a desire to accept the ethical principles of other frameworks for conviction.

In this way, they do not care about names that refer to specific religious beliefs, like "Catholic," "Baptist," "Hindu," "Muslim," or "Buddhist" itself. Buddhists do not seek the extension of their association, nor do they attempt to convince people of a particular belief.

Instead, they offer the answer if they are asked. The Buddha encourages people to be mindful and interested and this is how Buddhism can be seen as a form of living in perspective of wisdom instead of confidence. You must be energized to learn the specific teachings that are taught by the Buddha.

The Buddha's teachings are vast to that they are so extensive in the sense that they was able to evolve into various forms of Buddhism. Whatever the case we must not lose the focus of the matter in the present. At present you are able to learn deeper into the lessons of Buddhism that you will find out more about in the next section.

Before turning the page, take a moment to recall the words from Buddha. Buddha himself. The key is to trust your mind not to take his advice, instead of examining your own understanding of his teachings. Only by doing so could you gain the ability to recognize the true meaning behind his remarks.

Chapter 2: The Teaching Of Buddhism

As a lot of people perceive Buddhism as a philosophical system instead of a religion, it's only natural that they have difficulty recognizing the significance of this practice. However, even though Buddhism does not believe in the worship of a God and doesn't revolve around beliefs, doesn't necessarily mean that it doesn't have the potential to improve your spirituality. In fact , it's quite contrary.

The spirituality that is inherent in practices of Buddhism is at the heart of the ultimate spiritual awakening. For Buddhists living an enlightened life is taking the right path that can end all suffering and penetrate within yourself to help you perceive and comprehend the world around you. In order to achieve that, you must develop compassion and the ability to discern. The spirituality of Buddhism is in the pursuit of these values.

We are accustomed to looking for the unanswerable in the world of religion. How did the world get made? Does the universe have a definite existence? Is the soul distinct from the body? What happens when we die? For many of us, getting that answer signifies that we've reached the point of no return. However, Buddhists have a very differing view on this issue. According to them, the meaning of the word "spiritual" isn't about the waste of your time, energy and perhaps your entire life, in the search for these spiritual truths. The spiritual is in the present and now by the way you're actualizing the life you are asking the questions. Spirituality's core is not what you think you'll see in the world around you, but rather what you do with it and how you live your life. To be genuine, compassionate and intelligent, we don't have to resolve these metaphysical questions. All we need is to be aware of the existence that we're living.

Don't interpret this in a negative way. Buddhism might not be a religion that believes in God however, it does not deny the existence of God. It does not have any disagreements with other religions. It also does it require you to abandon your previous faith to become a Buddhist. It is simply a belief that the primary goal of the spiritual and holy life is to end the suffering.

When Buddha realized the meaning of being awake, he began his goal of helping others become enlightened. His first teachings laid the foundations for Buddhism that we are familiar with to this day.

The Three Signs of the Being

After achieving the art of the art of meditation Buddha realized that all that exists in the physical world has three traits. These three traits are referred to by the name of three indicators existence, and form part of the most important teachings of Buddhism:

Annica - the change. Buddha taught that nothing in the world is forever and that everything is subject to change. According to Buddha that all things cease to exist and all things are always in flux and change. Think about it for a second. Your life is constantly evolving. You're not the same person you were just a few years ago. you're older, more educated and maybe wiser. But the person you're now is still in a state of change, and in the next few years the person you are now will be completely different. Buddha taught that it's impossible to create something that will remain for ever, as we all are constantly changing.

DUKKAH - suffering. The suffering of a being is the inability of the being to stay content. The way we live our lives is not perfect and nothing we can get from the physical world can satisfy us. If you take a moment to think about this, you'll realize how true. We all go through our lives wishing for things that we do not have. When we finally get what we has been our dream all our lives, we're happy for a time however it's not a feeling that lasts or is a lot of depth. We are then able to find another thing to be wishing for and we continue to suffer.

AnnATA - Impersonality. This refers to the manner that the Buddhists examine human beings. They do not see any personal qualities within themselves, since Buddha taught that there is no permanent thing within our bodies. There isn't a thing as a soul because we are an accumulation of elements that include form, consciousness perception, mental activity...

The Four Noble Truths

Four noble principles form the essence of Buddhism and its fundamental tenet. Buddha did not believe in the the afterlife, which is a heaven-like space in which those who have lived an ideal life on earth are destined to. He believed in the pain which people are being trapped in. But, he also believed in the possibility of escaping this trap.

The 1st Noble Truth

Everyone suffers and live the life of a person who is filled with sadness. What exactly is it that causes suffering? It is a sign of aging, birth or illness, dying, feeling discontent.

The 2nd Noble Truth

The reason we suffer is nothing more than our desires and needs. It could be the need to be (where the notions of birth, aging as well as illness and death are part of) or the desire to attain something tangible and/or material.

The 3rd Noble Truth

The only way for anyone to get out of the cycle of suffering is to acknowledge it is not possible to find a soul inside us. This is done by denying the need to be, or any other desire.

The 4th Noble Truth

Only way for you to be successful in removing desires is to follow the eightfold way.

The Way of Inquiry

There is no such thing as a blind faith. Buddhism doesn't have the reputation of a religion that would insist that you put your faith blindly in something or somebody. In fact, it has been Buddha himself who influenced the method of investigation. According to Buddha the Buddha, nobody should ever do something or believe that something is truthful or based on an opinion. No matter if it's from an elder , traditional, academic, authority or even the priest, one should keep an open mind regarding everything.

Beware of the dangers of constructing your faith on unsupported grounds, Buddha warned strongly against blind faith. At the core of Buddhism is the method of investigation. Before making an idea, believing in someone or something or forming a opinion about someone or something the first thing you must do is research. For the moment, one needs to remain open and be tolerant.

The Eightfold Path

The eightfold path, or the middle way' is considered to be the most significant tool in Buddhism that symbolizes everything that is right. Only when people truly decide to follow the eightfold path will be closer to their authentic self, let go of the desires, and keep free of the illusions.

Here are eight of the best perspectives that will make you happy and bring your everlasting happiness:

1. Right View

2. Right Intent

3. Right Speech

4. Right Action

5. Right Livelihood

6. Right Effort

7. Right Mindfulness

8. Right Concentration

The initial two steps of this process - having the right perspective and intention will allow a person to truly transform their appearance.

Third, fourth and the 5th step, the proper words, actions and life style - will aid a person in living in their commitments and avoid behaviors that are a cause for concern.

The three final steps - the right amount of effort focus, mindfulness, and effort can assist a person achieve the highest level of happiness and live their life in peace.

The Karma

Understanding Karma is among the main tenets of Buddhism. Although this practice was common in India prior to the time Buddha was born however the Buddha was Buddha who was able to finish and develop this concept. Its explanation on karma has been in a constant manner and is respected today.

The idea of Karma is a vast subject and there's a lot to discuss it. However, I'm going describe it in a specific way to make it understandable. In short, karma means action. Karma is a thing that is the consequence the actions we take. According to Buddha the Buddha, there are no random events or coincidences in the world. We are the designers of our lives, and our actions are reflected back like boomerangs. If we commit a sin and we are punished, we'll get negative consequences, but if we are good, goodness is bound to come our way. Nobody can avoid karma as it is shaped by our actions.

If we made a mistake in the past does not mean we are likely to live a life, which will be of similar proportions to our previous mistake. Buddha believes in Karma in a strong way, but He also believed in being in a position to lessen the impact. It's inevitable, but its severity could be reduced. Consider, for instance, lemons. If you squeeze an entire lemon and drink the juice, what would it taste like? What if you were to squeeze a lemon into an ice-cold glass and then drink it? Which of the two was more flavorful? You could have drunk lemon's juice in both situations but drinking it in combination with water resulted in the opposite effect. Imagine karma this in this way. Karma is essentially a reflection of what you give out. If you release negative things, you'll get negative results, however when you do positive things, the outcomes will be beneficial for you.

The Rebirth

Rebirth, as the word implies it is being birthed again. The traditional Hindu explanation of the concept of reincarnation refers to the idea that the spirit, or the atman may be born several times. While Buddhists believe that rebirth is possible, this idea becomes a bit more ambiguous in this case, since as we've said previously, Buddha was known to preach the concept of no soul or atman. If there's an absence of souls, who is Reborn? It isn't necessarily the body since it's just the sum of its components.

There are several types that make up Buddhism and each of them offers a distinct explanation of what rebirth within Buddhism signifies. The most popular one is the one of Theravada Buddhism that is deeply linked to the way Buddha saw death and life. He believed there was some kind of causal link between the two states. According to him, the causal connection is in reality, the concept of karma. Karma influences the birth of a baby and the child does not look the same that was born previously, but is not significantly different from the person who passed away.

Theravada Buddhism teaches that in the creation of an individual, there's more than the father's sperm or eggs of the mother. It's Karma's energy well. If a person dies, the karma they created endures and results in a new birth.

Other schools consider this is not of karma, but rather the mind of the person who lives on after death and leads to rebirth.

However, Buddha believed not only in this particular realm, but also throughout the world. He believed that all of us species - animals, human beings insects. We are all connected and that we can change our form in the event of death. He believed that this helps us be more compassionate and helps us become better people.

Buddha was also said to recollect his previous life. Certain monks also have achieved this by performing meditation.

BOTTOM LINE

The essence of Buddhism doctrine is that one endures constant suffering. Because of the act of the cycle of rebirth, people are being pursued by their karma. They will never truly be happy until they have eliminated all empty desires from their lives and embrace the doctrine of no-soul. This is the only way to truly realize their true potential. The blissful state is known as Nirvana. It is the state that occurs when one gains an understanding of the truth and is free of pain (rebirths). Nirvana will be your ultimate aim of life. If a person achieves Nirvana, the cycle of rebirth ceases and they are able to be on earth in complete equilibrium.

Chapter 3: How To Have The Right Thought, Right Speech And Right Understanding

Mindfulness isn't as much a response rather than an action since Mindlessness is the reverse of mindfulness. It is typically, the guttural responses we all experience to the daily stimuli we encounter. If we're not aware enough, we often share things with others that we would rather not. If it's via the use of words or non-verbal communications, we should be mindful and stop to consider what that we are putting out onto the world. This is an essential tenet in Buddhist philosophy.

Contrary to what political experts might have you believe the ability to communicate isn't a privilege which is only given to those who are gifted and ignored by some. We are not living in a society that makes certain people with natural speaking abilities and the rest relegated to using teleprompters. Effective communication, like everything else in our life, is a skill and it doesn't matter if we master this skill when we're aged 4 or 40 years old, it's not a matter of. It's all that matters is to get it trained. What better time to begin then now!

The first step in developing a mindfulness is to ensure that you're in the driver's seat in your personal conversations. That means you must keep your focus when you speak. Don't let your thoughts wander to thoughts that do not have anything related to the topic issue at hand keep your attention always on the issue that is at hand. It is essential to focus on what other people are saying, as well as the words coming from your mouth.

Concentration will allow you to think through how to present your arguments and suggestions towards the individual.

The ability to think clearly allows you to be clear in your discussions and lets you become as a chess master who is able to anticipate the moves of the other player ahead of time and customize your responses and comments to be relevant to the issue in question.

Another thing that anyone who is practicing "right speech" realizes is the value of silence in their speech. For those who are Buddhist it's the effect of the non-declaration of silence that differentiates the most significant aspects of our lives. If you're practicing what is known as the "right speech", silence is the most powerful punctuator that helps us clarify our thinking. Between every brilliant thought you've got there must be an insulating silence so that your thoughts don't get unclear and undefined.

A lot of us think we are accustomed to the power to be silent in our speeches and we often ramble between disjointed ideas and then the following. We are known for long-winded arguments that appear to leave us nothing but we're out of breath! If we do not allow a conscious pauses in our speeches and we are prone to introducing items into our speech that shouldn't be in the first place.

The addition of unnecessary or excessive details muddles the message we want to convey. A person who rambles from one thing in a disorganized manner to another is a person who reacts to their personal subject matter can change at the slightest of impulses. In the most extreme case of this type of jumbled conversation is the people who appear to be unable to finish an idea, sometimes even forgetting what they were speaking about in the first instance!

I had a close friend who behaved like this before. When I ran into her in public spaces she would begin her conversation with one thought but then conclude with a completely different idea. She would let me leave me to shake my head in disbelief at the bizarre sounds I'd just encountered. In order to follow the Buddhist principle that is "right speech", we should ensure that our communications are clear and clear. Silence is the primary factor when it comes to doing this.

When you are compelled to go off in a direction that isn't yours You can stop this by using silence. When you have laid down the thought clearly in your conversation, stop and let silence perform its job, so that the words you've been saying is fully absorbed to you as well as the person you spoke it to. Let silence perform its role as the natural indentation between paragraphs of our conversation. In the absence of this space to breathe our words tend to flow through a confusing and messy chaos. It is essential to keep a pause between thoughts to allow us to absorb speech in a way that is effective.

In addition to allowing the silence of our voices, it is important to ensure that we make sure that we pronounce our words clearly and with low enunciation. It doesn't mean that you need to sound like you just played your tape deck at a halt! It's just that you should be sure to precisely convey your message without being overly formal or fast to ensure that anyone who listens can have the focus of the message you're trying to communicate to them.

Alongside with the proper kind of speech is the appropriate level of understanding. When you are able to comprehend people and the circumstances they're in, you must be able to avoid being too easily affected by their poor and unartful communication. People who aren't well-informed at the very least, are able to ruin our lives with only a few awkward phrases and words. As Buddhists are, we must be aware of these uninspiring musings on the internet on faith.

In the case of those who can hurt you by their words, and while there are occasions when these verbal smacks and psychological daggers may be directed at you in a deliberate manner but, most of the time it is likely that they were not intended and are merely a evidence of another's poor emotional intelligence and inability to express their thoughts in a constructive and positive manner. The term that is often used to describe people who are unhappy and chaotic in their communication is the term "toxic person".

For the majority of us, our normal tendency is to avoid people who are toxic at all costs and, like if they carry the disease, we would like to eliminate them immediately and quarantine completely. However, according to one of the most influential Buddhist philosophers to ever speak on the issue the Vietnamese's Thich Nhat Hanh informs us that to attain "right understanding", we cannot avoid people who are negative. Instead of avoiding them it is better to be able to accept and understand. In addition, we should take part in what he calls "Deep Listening".

If we encounter people who are toxically affected in this way, we can demonstrate our self-defined "right understanding" by hearing the individual from a neutral and detached viewpoint. When we listen without being caught up in the person's anger and ranting it is possible to gain an understanding that is rational of the root causes of this person's distress.

We become the conscious observer of the root causes of their anxiety, and as consequently, are in a far better position to assist them to deal with their issues. When you develop these skills, you become a more compassionate and generous person. This will return you into your "Right Thought" of Buddhism that allows you to become compassionate and caring about people in need.

Chapter 4: The Four Noble Truths

Four noble truths are the most basic and easy of all of the principles Buddhist philosophy. Knowing these four truths are essential to understanding the whole Buddhist philosophy. The tradition states that the four truths were realized by Buddha when he was contemplating under the shade of a Bodhi tree.

In the first two truths Buddha acknowledges the issue. Third truth: Buddha suggests the solution. In the fourth, he reveals to us the best way to deal with the issue.

The following are the 4 main principles of Buddhist philosophy.

1. "Life means suffering"

Some might view this idea as skewed However, Buddha is simply reiterating the truth that living means to be suffering.

Buddhists believe that this is an accurate conception of life because suffering can take many varieties. People can be suffering physically emotionally, mentally emotionally, or even spiritually. It's an inevitable part of our lives and something we can't truly avoid.

The primary types of suffering Buddha identified were suffering from old age, illness and death. But, it goes further than the above. The human condition isn't ideal. Humans are faced with challenges and issues which make life difficult.

The happiness you experience is brief and short-lived. So, we shouldn't be entangled to the pleasure of it. Because the world is in constant flux and change, these reasons for joy will eventually fade away. Similar to our motives for happiness as well as our loved ones, we us will one day die as well.

2. "The origin of suffering is attachment"

A second truth points to desires and affection as the root of suffering. Things we desire can be painful because they're temporary. It's not only the physical objects that disappear. Everything we perceive, including our personal notion about "self" will go away. Sometimes, our naivety of our personal attachment to our desires or dreams is what causes us to suffer. We attach ourselves to things for too long and it causes constant suffering over the long term.

3. "The cessation of suffering is attainable"

The third truth is a symbol of optimism that we can live a life free of suffering. The Buddhist name for the third noble truth refers to Nirodha or the letting go of desires. Buddha states that to achieve inner peace, one must become completely detached from your desires. This process of clearing oneself of all desires is the only route to attaining Nirvana. Nirvana is a state of release from worries, anxieties and suffering. The Nirvana state is one of unshakeable tranquility and a definite feeling of peace.

4. "The path to the cessation of suffering"

Buddha doesn't leave us in a dark corner. Through his teachings, Buddha shows us how to attain an enlightenment. As the 4th noble truth Buddha shows us how we can end our suffering. While this may sound easy to understand, other Buddhist doctrines go into more detail about how to go towards the state of enlightenment. He outlines the lessons of his journey through the eightfold route.

In simple terms Finding happiness is all seeking out the middle. It's about finding the right balance of self-sufficiency and self-mortification. When a person follows this path of self-improvement gradually the attachments, desires and cravings will vanish and, with them, anxieties, sufferings, and pains will disappear, too.

Chapter 5: Clearing The Path To Enlightenment

Buddhism encourages its followers to be active and to seek the truth, not only trust whatever the Buddha is saying. Though it can inspire people to consider their existence and the way of life, keep in mind it is Buddhism is not the way you choose to describe it. Buddhism is a discipline that includes an array of doctrines and practices that set it apart from other faith systems. Knowing what the Buddha was teaching through his teachings a crucial aspect of the practice. For instance, one of the fundamental principles in Buddhism includes one of Four Noble Truths as enumerated in the preceding chapter. To become a disciple of Buddha is to comprehend these principles deeply not just on a conscious level, but also on the spiritual level in which the Buddha taught it. These insights will help pave the way to becoming transformed. What is it that you may think? Yes, it can be done, since, as Buddhist followers want to remind us that and the Buddha can be considered a normal human being. If he was able to attain a state of enlightenment What would stop others in experiencing this same kind of state of consciousness? What are the steps to clear the way towards awakening and thus toward peace within? Below are simple discussions on the basis to Buddhism as well as its noble Truths. You might want to look through other books on Buddhism to further enhance knowledge of the principles. As a novice who's just beginning your quest to understand Buddhism I would like to think this will suffice to get the journey towards your goal of inner peace.

The first step to awakening:

The first step on the path to enlightenment, and thus inner peace as per Buddhism is acknowledging "Dukkha." Scholars of Sanskrits and Pali language translated this word to mean roughly "suffering" so the first noble truth could literally refer to "life is suffering." But Buddhist adherents would stress that the word "dukkha" can also refer to distress, illness and discomfort. The acknowledgment of suffering as a part of life may appear to be a negative view to the outsider. But, if you look deeper into the words of Buddha the Buddha also speaks about happiness and joy. What does understanding about the "truth about suffering or dukkha" actually mean in an Buddhism sense? It is quite simple, when you realize that life is made up from "dukkha" or sufferings, and also happiness, one can be aware of the cause for his difficulties. Being aware can be half the battle as they say.

Buddhism does not adhere to the mere repetition of doctrines and is primarily about figuring out the way. If we acknowledge that life could be a source of sorrow, people are able to take action and not sulk under the illusion of peace which can be destroyed at any time. The Path towards enlightenment begins with acknowledgment. Similar to a doctor who diagnoses an disease, the patient must to recognize that he is suffering from pain and inform the doctor about the discomfort. Only after determining what is the cause of the disease is the doctor able to recommend a treatment that will ease the symptoms of illness. This is like knowing the primary noble truth of Buddhism.

The second step to awakening:

Once a person has accepted that there exists a problem or discontent The next major Buddhism belief is about the root of dukkha or , in Sanskirt/Pali, dukkha samudaya, which is described as "dukkha is caused by desire." What is the desire that leads to suffering or dukkha?

Cravings , or tanha in Pali literally refers to "thirst." In the first sermon of the Buddha the Buddha talks about "cravings for sensual pleasure, cravings for becoming and cravings for non-becoming." These tanhas are associated with craving or greed. A good example of sensual cravings is when you desire to take a bite of a burger and you want to eat it even though you're not hungry. Desires to become are on the other hand, and can be described best by the people's desire for power or a desire to become famous. A desire for not being famous can be seen by the desire to rid of something until it becomes an obsession, for example, the destruction of something or in an easy way of getting rid pimples.

Here I must mention that in Buddhist tradition teaching about the noble second truth doesn't hinder the person from enjoying the things he desires or seeks. The most important thing is to examine the causes of clinging to or being tied to these cravings. If there is a notion that is based on "me" versus other beings there is a tendency to focus on oneself and is, according to Buddhism is the reason for endless cravings. If you think of "me" rather than "we" then we have an urge to safeguard ourselves. oneself is something which should be kept safe, content, to be indulged. If we continue to hold to this view in accordance with the Buddha the Buddha, then other desires or desires will arise like anger, fear, or jealousy.

Another noble fact informs that dukkha is a result of desire to protect one's "self." As long that our thoughts shift away from "us" to "me" and when one is able to separate himself from all other things desire and cravings will persist. The second noble truth connects to the concept that is "Karma" in Buddhism, that can be misunderstood. Karma is an Pali word that is translated to mean "volition action." The doctrine of Buddhism says that when our actions are accompanied by three poisons (greed anger, lust, and insanity) The result of our deeds or Karma is more dukkha, sufferings as well as pain or stress.

Three steps to illumination:

The third and most important truth the basis of Buddhism is the ending of suffering. In a very basic sense the ending of suffering, or dukkha, lies in the release of our cravings. However, if we comprehend the two noble truths thoroughly and deeply, we will realize that letting go isn't only about forcing ourselves to stop our desires or declaring, "I won't crave anymore." This method is not effective because the reasons that lead to our desire are in existence. The reasons behind desires or cravings is being experienced in the world, in the way the initial noble fact instructs us. In Buddhism there is the notion of renunciation. But renunciation in the Buddhist sense isn't just to throw away or eliminate things, such as to say, "I do not want it or I do not crave it." The concept of renunciation is the natural shedding of things that tie us to dukkha due to insight. This is why, in Buddhism the emphasis is placed on contemplation, meditation and an in-depth study.

The Buddha says to his followers that in order for suffering to be over one must recognize the root of the pain or the desires and must engage in a deep, conscious effort to think outside of oneself and let go of these desires. If a person recognizes that his cravings are the reason for his suffering and has gained the insight into these cravings that are gone at their own will. This is a natural process that can only occur through an in-depth investigation and understanding. If one is able to understand the nature of dukkha as well as cravings, and comes to an understanding of the effects it has on his life, as per Buddha the dukkha fire is snuffed out. This is known as"Nirvana" or the state known as "Nirvana" or the extinction of thirst. Note that Nirvana does not resemble an imaginary heaven, as the imagination of those who are new to this Sanskrit language. The most accurate meaning of the word "nirvana" means "to extinguish" like to put out the flame.

The Buddhist sense fire isn't synonymous with flames. What we perceive as a flame is the connection of the fire to fuel. But fire is present, though in a different form in the absence of fuel. The Buddha was a great Buddha told those he taught that flame of dukkha is gone or vanish by letting go of attachment to the desire. If we are able to release these desires with an natural process of letting go or renunciation. The person suffering, or experiencing dukkha, transforms. This new self is different from the typical self we encounter in our daily lives that it can't be imagined from the common experience, according to the Buddha.

Step four of enlightenment:

4. The noble fourth truth, also known as the reality of the way to free people from suffering is to be explored in the following chapter. At this stage that the fourth noble fact will provide us with what "how" or the action to take to be free of suffering as well as pain, suffering and distress, and ultimately achieve nirvana, or the end of all cravings and finally inner peace.

I'd like to go over more in depth the noble four truths that make up the basis of Buddhism provides in a simple way, suitable for an uninitiated student of learning the Buddhist doctrines. First Noble Truth: The First Noble Truth is akin to diagnosing or identifying of the presence of a disease. The second explains the cause of the illness. The Third assures that there is a solution and recommends the cure.

It is important to emphasize that, beneath the truths preached by Buddhists there are many layers of wisdom on the nature of the self, of life existence, existence, and death and, of course, the notion of suffering. The Buddha is not content with requiring his followers to be blind in his teachings and beliefs, but rather to research the teachings, comprehend them and evaluate their validity in relation to the experiences of one's own. This method of discovery, insight analysis, and understanding that makes up Buddhism.

Chapter 6: The Mind Of A Buddhist

Being a Buddhist involves a lot in mindfulness. As you become at one with the mind you will experience the three main purposes of the practice that are learning how to train and freeing your mind.One among the many crucial actions to know your mind is to understand what we're made of. In most cases, a quick review of your surroundings may assist in this, particularly in the event that your journey takes longer. It is possible to ask yourself questions as simple as,"What is happening to your body?"This allows you to feel more in control or aware of the surroundings.

The process of training the mind in thinking of these innovative thoughts obviously, will be challenging. This isn't a quick shift, but an ongoing process is a challenge to push through. It is imperative to get your brain trained to think in a completely different way. One of the best ways to begin the process is to train and demonstrate the ways to be kind. The process of releasing your mind is the process of letting go of the stress that are a part of your daily life. The constant worry and stress needs to be eliminated and your mind should be able to move to more meaningful thoughts. The process of getting rid of this negative energy can be achieved by meditative. When you are in the most profound state of meditation, and by observing your thoughts, you'll be able identify what negative thoughts are manifesting within your life. When you realize this, you will be able to begin get rid of these troubles. The freedom of your mind will allow you to allow yourself to enjoy the freedom you've always wanted.

The 3 steps to Buddhism allow you to release your body into a higher level of enlightenment. One of the first steps, recognizing your mind, can be difficult to grasp to first.Due to the awe-inspiring amount of thoughts that we experience every day it can be difficult to discern which ones need to be addressed and what isn't. To be able to fully comprehend the state of mind it is necessary to be in a state of quiet. This lets the mind see issues even when a lot of quiet isn't taking place. Even a small amount of silence could alter the course of your day. Once you have a clear mind is clear, you can take action based on your new perspective. You'll know the choices you make and the reasons behind decisions.

The brain is comparable to the shape of a sponge. It takes in all the events that occur in your daily life, and then stores it for a long time. As an example, you're on your TV, and you see a commercial that shows beautiful, slim people.For many individuals, we look at ourselves with these people. We're not as beautiful or as slim as their counterparts and we judge ourselves in the same position. Your mind is simple to repair and transform to create a new one It's crucial to gain control of your thoughts ahead of other media outlets. In this day and age it is essential to be kind to people around us is important.Being friendly to others can help shape us to be better individuals. It's not easy on you or your body. You will face many issues that you didn't previously have. You might realize that the majority of your stressors had to do only one person, object, or place. When you have dealt with these issues, is when you begin to train yourself to deal with these issues differently.It's essential to keep in mind that dealing with these issues in a calm manner will leave you on positive ways. If you are more stressed out about managing your stress, your issues will only grow more complex. To achieve an unwinding state when you meditate, it is important to be able to approach it with a sense of peace. The practice of meditation shouldn't be overdone or require an excessive amount of concentration put into it. The main goal is to focus on relaxing your body. The rest will be revealed when you're done. A moment of relaxation is now over and educating your mind is much more manageable.

The process of releasing your mind involves letting go of the thoughts of negativity that take over your thoughts. In the initial step of knowing your mind, you'll discover where the stress is originating from. This will help you let them go and get rid of negativity thoughts.These negativity thoughts keeping you from what could truly be. Everyone deserves to be something we've always wanted towards be.If Buddhism hadn't been introduced to the lives of your loved ones, then there might be a myriad of other hurdles that you'd have to face. After you've learned some things about Buddhism and its benefits, you'll be able to see that meditation is extremely beneficial. The goal of Buddhism is to allow yourself to be as unrestricted as it is possible. This means avoiding unnecessary worries to consume our daily lives. It's not an easy task to rid your heart and mind of any kind of. It requires a lot of practice, time and dedication to thoroughly cleanse the body and mind of the"poison"life could inject you with. Once you are able to let go you will find it much easier to learn how to train yourself. Like you, your body requires upkeep too.

Chapter 7: The Eight-Fold Path

The eightfold path is an approach to end your suffering. It is a description of the requirements for you to reach an enlightened state. The state of enlightenment is one of mind that is where there is no suffering. It is a state of peace and tranquility that is an image of pure happiness. Let's take a examine the eightfold path that can be the path to true happiness.

Right understanding: It's about achieving the real purpose of your life. When you understand your goal for your existence, then you will strive to accomplish this purpose, and this will provide you with satisfaction and a sense of purpose.

Ideal Aspiration fact warns against the pursuit of the illusion of nothingness. It is important to realize that the goal of life is to do the things that are meaningful to you and to stop suffering for you and for others.

The Right Way: This portion of the eightfold path aims to demonstrate that you have to put in the effort in your life to be truly blissfully happy and enlightened. It enjoins you from making reasons to not do something, and is designed to inspire you to act. If you have something that you have to do, simply perform it.

The Right Way: Buddha realized that our tongue can be a trigger to many negative experiences humans go through. In his teachings about the eightfold path, the Buddha is trying to dissuade individuals from engaging in negative speech. The eightfold path is to speak truthfully with compassion and kindness. Remember that hurtful the words you speak can be a source of hurt to others, but also to yourself.

Good Conduct: You must to ensure there is a logical connection between your behavior and the values you hold. Life is guided by proper values.

Right Livelihood: It's beneficial to earn a living honestly. It is difficult to earn an income in the way that it makes others be hurt.

Right Mindfulness The moment you are at your awareness is put to examination. This element of the eight-fold method is to ensure that , as you go through life you are aware of the significance of being present in the moment. It states that the present is crucial and the highest point of your awareness and awareness of what's happening in the world around you. Avoid tying your attention with the past or in the future to be. Take in the reality of the moment and live a life that demonstrates your awareness to the present.

The Right Focus: Buddhism seeks to help you increase your alertness, concentration, and awareness through meditation. Zen Buddhism draws a lot of inspiration from this aspect of the eightfold path. It has been proved that such a state of mind is the most effective method to attain enlightenment and happiness. What exactly is the process of enlightenment? However, certain Buddhist texts have implied that enlightenment involves the realization of a momentous realization. It's not the essence of the concept. It is the understanding of the basic factual information that influences our lives. It's about knowing the facts and applying the knowledge so that you're always kept in mind of the facts. Therefore, this knowledge is translated into action and thought the correct actions.

Realization

Realization is a reference towards the Buddhist realization that everything arises from nothing. there is nothingness that creates the dimensions and forms of our everyday lives that are often misinterpreted and definitely not satisfactory.

How the Four Noble Truths Relate To Inner Peace

The fundamental principle of these four truths of wisdom is the creation of a solid, stable person with an inner mind that is filled with peace and happiness.

Inner Peace

Four noble principles begin with the truth of lifeand the cause of suffering. This is an attempt to alleviate the anxiety which are usually the result of ignorance. When you accept the reality, you enter an acceptance state. This is the precursor to an increase in the stability of your brain.

True Happiness

A second truth reveals and provides you with the reasons that cause suffering. Once you have a clear understanding of the causes of suffering , you'll be capable of separating your thoughts from it and cut off the ties you have to those factors. Happiness is achieved by getting rid of the root cause of suffering. The main cause, of course is, as you've guessed, is clinging and desire. When you look beyond the physical desires, you are free from the bind of discontent. It is possible to deal with discontent when you follow the guidelines of the eight fold route. This formula can be used to cut down the effect of discontent, which is commonly referred to as the satisfaction is not a problem.

Mindfulness: A Source of Your Inner Peace and Happiness

Mindfulness is the foundation for practicing Zen Buddhism. It is achieved by the practice of meditation. Like the name implies, it's a philosophy designed to bring your mind to the correct direction to attain complete peace and happiness.

How do you define mindfulness?

Mindfulness can be defined as an ongoing and total consciousness of present. This is the process of recognizing the most fundamental truth. Mindfulness helps train your mind to recognize what is most important in your life, the ultimate truth. Get rid of your emotional and mental baggage by practicing mindfulness.

In fact, as discussed in previous chapters practicing Zen is based to these four truths as well as the eightfold path. Mindfulness is a reflection of the same.

The focus of practicing mindfulness lies in recognition of the normal mind is prone to wander around without restriction. It is prone to speculate, and then gets trapped in problems. As a result, emotions develop and your body and mind become unstable.

Mindfulness realizes that to achieve true happiness your mind must be free. So, it is essential to maintain a calm, calm mind to achieve inner happiness and peace.

How to Get Inner Peace from the Practice of Mindfulness

Mindfulness can be described as a sort of physical location that you must visit within your head. You go to, look around the landscape, and pinpoint important places. Mindfulness is triggered by the present moment rather than fears anxiety, worries and fears that remind us of our inexperienced mind.

Since we think of the mind as a physical location, we can move around the space according to the circumstances. We can change the scenery and places within this physical space according to the needs that are in the present. It is also known as the correct mental state. It is a fact that we face difficulties every day. There are times when we face the task of making difficult decisions. When we train in mindfulness we can shift our minds into a position where it is simpler and easier to take a decision.

When we are able to move our minds in that manner; to the places that are suitable for specific tasks the mind is also in self-perpetuating capabilities. It can adjust itself without needing any conscious effort to be attuned.

Mindfulness can lead to inner peace and happiness as it's a method for helping you become aware of the things that truly are. It doesn't create or conceal. The result of this awareness is satisfaction. We are all aware that being content is the precursor to feeling happy whether it's a long-lasting kind of happiness as it is by mindfulness or through the superficial and temporary nature of pursuits for material wealth.

Mindfulness is a path to a state of complete and lasting happiness , which comes out of inner tranquility. Peace is not the same as peace. It is caused by the inability to accept the current situation we are facing.

We've talked a lot about the possibility of obtaining true and long-lasting happiness with Zen Buddhism especially by realizing the four noble truths as well as the eightfold path. But, what does happiness mean? Happiness is a desirable state. This is why it's difficult to define it to a specific definition. Ideal is a level so high that it's almost impossible to attain using common and normal methods.

We seek to know what happiness is through the many manifestations we encounter in our lives.

The types of happiness

Happiness can be defined on one level as changing desires and sensual pleasures that occur in life. Mindfulness as a practice of Zen Buddhism regards this as the most depressing type of happiness that is devoid of any of the qualities that make it an eternal value. A lot of people are caught in the search for this type of happiness throughout their lives, but with no or no success; it is a miserable form of happiness that is constantly changing shape.

Another form of happiness that offers the most stable foundation for peace is abstinence. This is the type of joy that can be experienced when you practice the teachings of Buddhism. It's about letting go of the desire for pleasures and things of the material world and focusing instead on spiritual growth and growth. This is the type of satisfaction that the practice of Zen Buddhism and the application of the doctrines of Buddha as embodied by the Four Noble Truths provides you with. When you let go of clinging to and worldly pleasures, you are rid of the cycle of suffering. In turn, you will begin to find peace within yourself and with the world. Giving is a type of abandonment. If you are generous your time and energy towards the world that surrounds you. You are free from the desire to be focused on your own needs and the causes of materialism. Learn to give in order to relieve others of stress, strain and physical pain.

The most blissful form of happiness is when one reaches levels of spiritual awakening. This is only achievable through studying and implementing the principles taught within the 8 steps on the eightfold path. When you are able to absorb the lessons of the eightfold path, you're transported to a higher level which allows you to clearly identify the cause of your discontent. You go straight to the root, then uproot it and eliminate it. After that, you'll be able to remain at peace with your will and a peace of mind which is unaffected through the forces that cause discontent.

Mindfulness helps you go step-by-step throughout the classes. It offers everything for everyone. If you're unable to see past the material aspects of happiness, studying, reading and practicing of mindfulness allows you to discover and develop the skills to achieve this kind of material happiness.

However If you're prepared to endure and find out the meaning of what happiness and peace is, then you can absorb the first three noble truths. This will allow your perception to be transformed. The process is deliberate. First, you are made to understand that there is suffering. After that, you have the chance to discover the root of the suffering. You can now discern how your desires are one of the primary causes of your suffering. endure in life. Thus, you will learn to control your cravings. The lower your cravings are, the less you suffer. This also means that the more cravings you experience, the worse your troubles will become.

The next step to true happiness is to end the cycle of suffering. If you are able to learn the skills of mind to end Dukkha the next step is to begin to ascend higher levels of understanding what life like. This is the 3rd noble truth. It aims to help you get rid of suffering by knowing its mechanisms and the areas of intrusion. It is a way to let go of the illusion of happiness and set off on an adventure to find true happiness. This journey will culminate in the eightfold path, the most effective formula to end suffering caused by unsatisfaction.

The eightfold pathway is a slow path that leads you to the last journey of awakening. The journey to enlightenment is not a single event. It is a realization that is revealed through the study and application of the principles that are outlined by the Eight Steps of the eightfold path.

You can begin with where you are, and then continue to build upon what you already have to be (a more stable person mentally). Also, the next step, which is called the 8 folds, allows you to be able to adapt the way you want to be.

Chapter 8: Different Schools Of Buddhism

There are various kinds of people around this world, Buddha devised different systems to meet the needs of different types of individuals. It was a smart choice since it means that Buddhism is applicable to all. The schools are identified in the following ways:

Theravada - Theravada was a school aimed at the elderly

If you're studying under this type of Buddhism you will be taught more about Karma as well as how it could influence your life. It also teaches you how to deal with the thought process and discover that thinking isn't something that is personal. It's just the passing of time. Because Buddhism is a way of teaching that all things are temporary, you can manage your thinking processes and use the notion that things will never last to help you get through times in which your brain is weak and your thoughts are in opposition to Buddhist principles. This type of Buddhism is practiced mostly throughout Thailand, Sri Lanka and in South East Asia and may be integrated into the teachings you receive during the retreat.

Mahayana This school is designed at bringing you to the point of the realm of enlightenment, and then to apply this enlightenment to benefit of other. People who are Buddhist monks are able to follow this type of Buddhism however it's not just restricted to the monks. In this kind of Buddhism you are taught all concerning The Eight Fold Path for a particular reason. It is because your words, actions and actions affect what happens around you. In this way, to some extent, you will achieve greater control and discipline of both your own and others' degrees of joy.

Schools that are part of this kind of Buddhism are also referred to by"the Northern Schools and the practice is prevalent in countries such as Asia, Japan, Tibet and Korea.

Vajrayana - also called The Diamond Way is aimed toward those who are seeking perfection in their minds. It requires lots of discipline and this kind of Buddhism includes the teachings of other forms of Buddhism practices mentioned above. Students who are taught in this type of Buddhism can see that the pursuit of perfection can only be accomplished by having an ideal mind. Therefore, mental discipline is crucial in this kind of Buddhism.

Zen Buddhism- Also covered under Mahayana This is the one type of Buddhism that you're likely to meet in the West, since it is a focus on meditation and enhancing your inner-self. It is the type of thing that most people are seeking out in meditation and is actually the type of practice employed by the Late Leonard Cohen. This kind of Buddhism involves a search in search of spiritual awakening. It is focused , but not centered. It's difficult to explain this to someone who is only getting started and, once you've stopped striving to achieve and instead focus on being Zen and being capable of letting off all of your preconceived ideas about life and instead focus on what's.

In this chapter the various forms of Buddhism and even though you could apply a portion of any of these ways of teaching You may also choose to concentrate on one that is a good fit for your needs. The most important thing at present is to develop an appreciation of the Eight Fold Path and that will be covered in the next chapter of the book. Also, you must learn how to meditate, as it is a crucial aspect of Buddhism and is covered in a separate chapter in the book.

What you'll be delighted to discover is that these kinds of Buddhism exist for a long time and have helped those who adhered to Buddhism philosophy in their quest for the best way forward in their lives.

Chapter 9: Who Was Buddha?

In the previous chapter we looked at the foundational tenets of Buddhism and the fundamental differences between Buddhism as well as other religions, and the things Buddhists do not adhere to. The next chapter we'll look at the person Buddha actually was, as it is vital to understand who you follow. Additionally, it is important to not forget that it's Buddha that you follow not monks or Buddhists who followed his death, who were reaffirming the belief system.

A brief history of Buddha

Buddha We know today as Buddha is actually the child of a king around the year 430 B.C. He was known as Siddhartha Gatama, and he lived a lavish life right from the beginning. He was never in a state of pain; or, it could be appropriate to declare that his parents did not let any pain befall him, and at the end of the day, he had no idea of what suffering is, what individuals feel during times of are suffering and what exactly is suffering. At the age of 29. Siddhartha was the prince from the ruling house in Nepal who was an ascetic wanderer later in his life after he realized the way that he had been living was unproductive and was based on false foundations. In the pursuit of knowledge what was important, he crossed boundaries. Before we get started in this article, it is important to be aware of one thing that there is a distinction in Buddhism in comparison to Hinduism. It's not a false factual suggests that Buddha is an Indian and an Indian and a Hindu prior to his departure exploring and looking for himself "self," but it is important to make it clear the fact that Hinduism and Buddhism are not the same thing.

The discovery that are a part of "self"" originated when the Hindu-priests ruled the area and there were strict rules within the realm. Everybody felt like being a rebel within themselves and began to search in search of"the "real" self, the "real" way of living. This was the time that Vardhamana was discovered as well and spoke about his beliefs. Jainism was born as the result. However, there is a distinction between them. Siddhartha recognized that asceticism was just as unsatisfactory as the lifestyle of luxury. He also realized that there must be an acceptable space between them that could be accepted by everyone, and eventually be able to become"the "enlightened one"--the Buddha.

What made Buddha an agitator?

It's not wrong to assert that the man was an outspoken rebel. He took a stand against the wishes of his father, and he held his position. If we go back to the past, we'll come to find out that at the time Siddhartha Gautama--the warrior's son of the King Siddhartha Gautama was born, the soothsayer had predicted that he could eventually become an renouncer, who would remove his self from the world of temporal. The king, upon hearing this, was terrified of ever let it happen, and consequently unaware of how nothing could alter his future. He attempted to grant Siddhartha all the comforts of life that would not allow him to become the absconder. But what happened was what happened regardless of how hard the king tried to his power.Siddhartha experienced the suffering. He was informed of it when riding for four horse rides.

What caused him to be suffering?

As mentioned earlier Siddhartha experienced suffering for the first time , when the chariots he rode on were the chariot for four rides. There were four types of sufferings he saw:

* Old age

* Illness

* Death

Siddhartha's concept of suffering

Prior to seeing all the above, Siddhartha believed that all the little pains and sufferings are reversible and that one can easily overcome these. Since his father King gave him everything he could ever want He believed that nothing could stand in the way of his happiness. However, as he experienced "old age," ,"sicknesses," and "death," he realized that these things are always present, and there is nothing that could be done to stop them. Like any other kind of pain, these sufferings weren't reversible, so he was driven to break out from his shell and explore the world.

What was his next move?

Then follows the next step where Siddhartha was able to take action to stand up for what which he felt he could be capable of seeing, while other people weren't. He decided to take action to change it. What did he did was quit the family of his spouse and son, named Rahula and went out in search of teachers, and attempted to break the shackles of renunciation in the forest all by himself and reaching to the level of being completely starving himself. He could not find anything that gave him the satisfaction of reaching the bottom, so the idea of reaching extremes, and after eating food, he laid down in a tree to contemplate. Once he had completed the most profound and effective practice of meditation, he recognized what was the root of his suffering and what was the cause and how to make yourself free of it. It was the moment of enlightenment that attained after a long meditation. What exactly was the thing he did that led him to this high point? The people who followed him became intrigued, and began to look for the motives.

What happened when the public became interested?

When they saw Siddhartha in a serene state, the whole world became attracted. They wanted to know what kind of treasure of life Siddhartha possess that allowed him to be so serene. Siddhartha himself was aware of what he needed to do in the next step by speaking, sharing his knowledge and helping everyone get to the right direction. After Siddhartha had been able to come out of his trance He began to tell his followers about the experiences he had during his meditation.

This was where his following began from the moment he began sharing his thoughts, starting at the time he was sharing his methods, and finally at the end of the day, he shared his experiences and lessons learned.

Chapter 10: "Holding On To Anger Is Like Drinking Poison And Expecting The Other Person To Die." - Buddha

Being angry is an emotion that is normal for humans, but tying yourself to it for longer than is necessary is not a good idea. The anger turns into hatred when you confine it for an extended period. If this happens then the only person suffering is you and not the person you are angry with.

A rage that is locked in your head isn't the most pleasant approach to living. The result is that it causes leaks in your energy and concentration. Through the day, you'll have moments of anger that come from the inside. It will be difficult to focus on your work, as your mind will be ruminating of the previous. The most difficult part of it is that it's all about anger. The anger fuels the anger. The more you consider the root of the problem of the anger, the more you are compelled to contemplate it. Then, you're not able to control your thoughts and, at this point, things begin to get out of hand. You're now a boat without steering wheels, incapable of setting sail in the direction you want. Once you've reached this point it's going to be difficult to get back in control.

This anger is to no purpose. If you really consider it, you'll forget about the anger later in life, which means that the time you are wasting in anger could be spent wisely, perhaps making the changes you want. The only thing that keeps you in the present is your mind's primal. If you're really pissed out, you won't desire to change your attitude You'd rather just be in a state of anger and stay angered. Think about the energy that you're wasting in the darkness. What are you doing with it? Wouldn't it be better to build your life the way you want?

If you are a victim of revenge, and desire, change it into happiness. That is instead of plotting to hurt someone else make a lifestyle where you feel fulfilled, happy and challenging. Happiness is the best reward. Why choose a path that causes more anger? If you opt for this path you'll only generate an even greater amount of this fiery anger that will result in more anger. Many people become addicted to it. It is true that anger can become addictive. The anger can make you forget all other things, it can create a burst of confidence that isn't as strong and, when you tell the person you love the things you think about her - and you spill the whole story out and really feel great afterwards or even satisfied. However, what occurs later? Once your mind is calmed, and you begin to regain consciousness, you feel regret creep into your heart, and depending on the intensity of your anger, you realize you've caused more harm than good for an instant of pleasure.

Although it may be difficult to bear the pressure but it's always better to let go of yourself and the person. If you are unable to accept forgiveness from someone in person, make the decision to forgive them in silence. When you forgive, it means you choose to let go of the hurt. As the hurt begins to wane and you are no longer feeling angry, there is no space for hatred, and you'll feel at peace with your life once more. If anger is a factor be able to accept it as common human reaction, but do not hold on to it. Doing this will swiftly turn your angry into hatred. The only one who suffers is you.

"All that we are is the result of all that we have thought." Buddha. Buddha

You may consider your thoughts to be a bit naive. You may think they're just something you do. Certain thoughts are entertaining, while other thoughts can cause hurt, but you should know that there's a lot of potential in these thoughts. The main difference that distinguishes us from animals the ability to switch focus, and to use our brains to decide between the right and wrong. If a predator is aware of the threat, its primary instinct is to either escape or to kill. When it does kill, it won't matter about what transpired. It doesn't matter if it's bloody and disfigured. Humans is, however is able to discern the right path and avoid wrong ones because of our logical brain. It isn't enough to just kill someone since you're able to see what the implications would be of this.

Thoughts are the basis of what makes humans; hence, it is important to not take them lightly. Your thoughts are literally and metaphorically thinking about what you are thinking about constantly. The key word is regularly. The more you consider something then the more you're weaving the webs of becoming exactly this. Another key word is the ability to focus. What you pay attention to regularly, whether daily, weekly or monthly, that shapes your perception slowly over time. If the reality you live in isn't what you'd like for it to become, then you've been paying attention to the wrong things or been thinking the wrong things. The more you concentrate on something, the greater the urge to take some kind of action. The thoughts build into the state of contemplation, while contemplation develops in focus. And then focus leads to actions. Action is a effective way to influence your mind. If you're choosing the wrong step that you're creating the mind of yours to become less strong as the long-term effects aren't what you'd like to see. For instance, if you are aware that you must consume healthy food however, you start to think of reasons (spending thoughts) then you'll begin to think about the negative things (focus) then you'll consider that unhealthy food that you are craving You will think that you'll be able to begin next week, and you'll tell yourself that you've been working hard recently and you're deserving of to take a break. And then, you'll decide to do the wrong issue: you'll go out to for a fast food restaurant even though you are aware that you have to eat a healthy diet. Thoughts > Focus > Action. Thoughts feed off one another to help form the focus. Focus fuels the desire to take action.

If there's one thing you're required to learn out of this book, it's that acting is the most effective method to change your thinking and eventually, your behaviour.

The majority of people do it reversed. They attempt to think positively about the possible outcome (step one thoughts) and attempt to connect their thoughts (step two: concentration) And hopefully, at some point, they'll be motivated enough to do something (step three: act). However, while it's still essential to keep track of what you are thinking (because it is what you believe regularly) it's virtually impossible to keep track of your thoughts every day. The key is to understand why you should begin with an idea when you can begin with action? It's going to take you a while to convince you to do something in order to complete the action however it is and the results will be awe-inspiring. When you make a decision your mind will be filled with thoughts. There is no need to manage it manually.

The key to happiness is making a decision about what you want in life and then making a commitment to it regardless of the outcome even if you do make an oath during the process. Put aside your thoughts and begin doing. It is a powerful thing to be taking action. You are the things you do every day However, actions will always prevail over thoughts, so you must force yourself to do something, since thoughts will be the next to follow.

"It is more beneficial to defeat yourself than beat a thousand opponents. This is the moment you can claim victory. It can't be taken away from you, neither by angels or demons, either in heaven or hell." -- Buddha

There will always always be someone more attractive, wealthier or smarter, more attractive, driven, or whatever you think of, than you. It's healthy to compete in a certain degree however, don't get consumed by the desire to be more successful than the rest of the world as you'll never achieve this aim. This kind of thinking either subconsciously or in conscious thought can cause a lot of self-doubt and anxiety particularly if you believe you're the best and you meet your ideal match or someone with more. For instance, if you place too much emphasis on looking good and better than others in your vicinity, what's going to happen if you run into someone with a better appearance than you? You'll doubt your self-worth and you'll be a saboteur to yourself.

Instead of competing against the others around you, begin trying to be your personal highest. Instead of fighting a thousand fights, just conquer one: yourself. If you can do this, you're increasing your self-confidence and most importantly of allis that you will no longer be comparing your self-worth against the other people who surround you. If you're not a charismatic person such as, for instance, asking the cashier about his day was may not be in your familiar zone. However, should you decide to do it you've just increased your personal limits and should be very proud of yourself for doing this, since you've beaten your previous self, your previous personal highest. This is where you can draw the self-worth you have built up from. Do yourself proud.

Be aware that there's an upper limit you need to be able to cross. It is not a good idea to be overwhelmed by the constant pursuit of perfection. As an example, you shouldn't be overwhelmed by going to the gym every day of the week in order to appear your best. Instead, find a place that you're happy about, and realize that you're good sufficient. It might be a little odd however, you're already sufficient in fact. There will never be insufficient, and If you expand whatever that may be your capabilities, you'll always be sufficient. Don't believe that you have to achieve a certain point in order to be adequate. It is only a waste of the most valuable resource you have that is time. The time you have on earth is short, and you may end up dying within the next week. Don't compare yourself with other people, and instead of trying to appear your best (because you feel you're not enough) be aware that you're already plenty and will always remain. This is something you must instill into your brain and Remind yourself that you're sufficient. Nothing is more frustrating than feeling like you're not worth it that should be an offence. In reality, you're far from being insignificant. If you look at all your ancestors , and the struggles they went through to bring you to the place you're at today (not to add that if one of the billions of people had taken a different decision and you didn't read this) You'll be able to see the value of who you are. Don't be scared if you're not like everyone else. Different is healthy. You're blessed with unique gifts, and it's the obligation to pass them on to the world before you go to sleep. If you do not take this step, you'll be guilty of the most serious crime of not understanding the value of who you truly are.

Although life is challenging at times, it's still something you must accept, a price you must be paid for being on earth. You may think that life isn't too difficult however, there are many who are suffering more stress. It is important to accept the life's challenges dealt to you and make use of your cards the best way you can. There's no reason to keep dreaming of a better life or being jealous of those with more. If you ever think you could have a better life, or perhaps that of someone who lives an extravagant lifestyle, remember the millions who are going to die in the next few days because they cannot find food or drink. Or maybe they find water, but it's too filthy, but it's okay since it's going to help the dryness in the throat disappear.

Don't be ashamed to have more because there's enough in the world to satisfy all. Being poor because you don't want be ashamed of having more than others does not help the world in any way. When you're enjoying all that life can offer by being happy, you're giving others the right to enjoy the same. You also have the ability to be more generous with other people, particularly those who do not have an improved future. This, in itself, is love.

Chapter 11: Learning To Be Humble

My journey began with studying humility. I believe it's the most ideal location for anyone who wishes to know more about Buddhism. If you don't have humility, you're incapable of seeing things from a the right perspective. Through it, you can see more clearly and become more compassionate when it comes to life. Thus, starting with humility is a great starting point. It's a good start. although you might have your own thoughts and beliefs about humility, we'd like to begin this journey in a straightforward manner against the background of nature. I often remind students that it is impossible to combat nature. It's the most powerful thing in the world, however, it also can reveal how humble and, in this instance this is the purpose we'll be using it for.

Find an area you believe to be breathtaking. The beach could be at sunrise or sunset. It could be high in the mountains or across a lake to an area of forest. Whatever the case you're looking for, make sure you visit the place in a time when there aren't any people as they can distract you from what's happening in your head. When you look at the beauty of the landscape before you, you'll be overwhelmed by its splendor. It is possible that you be struck by something that will assist you in knowing the essence of what Buddhism is about. You might be overwhelmed by the world that is in front of you. You might feel that you're as small as grains of sand. And you're right that we all are. But, if you did not possess all these tiny elements, like grains of sand, there'd have been no beach. So being small does not mean that you're small.

There is a reason to say that you don't have the money to visit a place that is breathtaking, however, in reality, you don't need to leave your home to experience the beauty of nature has to offer. Wake up at a reasonable time in the early morning and head out into the wild even before dew had vanished. Check for dewdrops on the cobwebs of plants and look up to observe how they look as diamond-like necklaces. Take a look at the way dew drops bend the grass blade, or watch the flowers pop to reveal the sun. Each of these moments can be very humbling as you are able to see that there is plenty more to the world than what you think it is. All your small issues disappear, and you're amazed by what you can see. This makes you be humbled by the beauty and grace of nature.

The importance of humility

Imagine that you were required to clean the floor. You believe that this isn't your job. So, if you are forced to clean your floors and you must, you can take it easy to get it completed. But, if you're conscious of the responsibility of washing your floor, you may make it an extremely spiritual experience. It's all about humility. When you complete a task with humbleness, you put the proper amount of effort and are cognizant of the job. You don't evade it, but instead you engage yourself in the process. It is a way of being aware of the passage of time but not in a manner that causes you to rush through every moment. Instead it allows you to be feel grateful for every moment, and helps you to achieve more through your awareness.

In a subsequent chapter, we'll discuss mindfulness, but it's as important in STEP 1 to develop the ability to be humble.

Being humble also helps you become more compassionate to other people. It is a sign that you are more open to listening and not think you are more valuable than that of the person speaking. You develop active listening, which means you're capable of figuring out the reasons people require compassion , not your critique. It helps you to look at things from a different perspective. It helps keep you from believing that yours is the only thing to do. It's not the case. The world is a vast space that is home to a variety of people and everyone has the same right to exist. When you practice humility that you don't judge others and you become more content because you will notice people attracted to you instead of being averse to you.

One of the humblest of human beings of the past century is likely to be Mother Teresa. She was a tireless worker for the homeless and provided assistance to those in need. She didn't give her needs a priority or even consider herself a priority. Some of the actions she accomplished were remarkable. It's hard to be fulfilled about the things you accomplish in life if it is the case that you perform it thinking that you are worthy of reward. If you decide to stop looking for rewards and perform the task because you're able to experience more spirituality inside than you can ever achieve from boasting about your accomplishments. Honest people are able to react when a need arises and continue to live their lives and be content that they have has made the lives of others a more comfortable. This is among the primary things you must integrate into your daily life in order to understand the principles that comprise Buddhism. These are guidelines to adhere to, but they're not a set of rules that are restrictive. In fact, they are guidelines that were put in place in order to let you live living life fully extent and to be the most successful person you could be. Remember, humility is the first step towards inner peace and happiness.

Chapter 12: In Depth Understanding Of Buddhism In Accordance To Daily Life

There are many variations between other religions as well as Buddhism. Many people don't understand Buddhism. In contrast to other religions, Buddhism bases its faith on the mind and not any gods. Pain and pleasure as well as evil and good as well as space and time existence and death, are meaningless to us unless we are aware of them, or our the thoughts we have about them. The question is whether God exists or doesn't exist, whether our existence is predominantly spiritual or physical and whether we live for just a few years or for ever--all these things are, according to the Buddhist viewpoint, secondary to the only fact about which we have absolute certainty in the presence of consciousness in every day life.

Being able to comprehend deeply in Buddhism is as simple to do as combing your locks, or looking up. The way to gain an understanding that is deep and profound is not by means of material objects, nor things that money can buy , but only through your thoughts... It's all in your head. In the modern age where the latest technology and gadgets are the ones that control our minds, this profound knowledge of Buddhism can ease our problems, something machines cannot accomplish.

Today, there appears to an absence confidence to God as more and more people are obsessed with things like money. Many believe that they can earn, work to accumulate and earn as much wealth as they wish to attain whatever they would like for. What's the feeling that comes from earning a large sum of money? Are you still not satisfied and want to find more? Truthfully I'm able to assure to you, money is an occasional pleasure and only something materialistic. Who would have thought that the enjoyment in the world was not endless? This is the kind of thing you can be able to experience in Buddhism You must be aware of the signs that will clearly and help you understand Buddhism. It is possible to become disinterested in the pursuit of spirituality or other spiritual pursuitsdue to the fact that "spirit" or consciousness reveals itself in everything we pay attention to. Everything is subject to. Whatever we direct our attention towards, we will be conscious of a new Presence that will be present throughout the day.

Our awakened consciousness can suffer but not the pain. We do not seek to escape reality, instead we become aware of its deeper significance. In Buddhism there is no way to be wrong. You will be able to get the things you desire, not to satisfy your desires as a human being, but to fulfill your soul. Take control of your emotions, as this is an important element that influences our decisions each day. This could be harmful and ineffective. There are research studies that show that emotions play a role in facilitating in our thinking and our actions and we sometimes do things which we aren't sure whether they're appropriate or not. Eliminate the fear in our heart and adopt a "can-do" attitude instead of "I will try" mentality. If something doesn't go as planned Rewrite your story and think about the things it could be differently and try another time, then ensure that you take a different approach. You can master the basics and aid you in gaining a greater comprehension of Buddhism.

Chapter 13: Practicing The Teachings

There are three main ways that Buddhists follow the teachings handed down by the Buddha hundreds many years ago. The first is by striving to live a moral life and strictly following the Buddhist doctrine. It is achieved by living your daily life in accordance with the Buddhist principles you were taught in the previous chapter and striving to constantly improve your life in this direction. Two other methods include yoga and meditation. The next chapter you'll be able to learn the details about both methods as well as receive some suggestions for getting to the point of starting.

Meditation

Meditation is described by it is the "practice in which an individual trains the mind or induces a mode of consciousness, either to realize some benefit or as an end in itself" (definition from Wikipedia). For Buddhism the advantage that one hopes to attain is the attainment of Nirvana.

To be able to meditate effectively, you must have complete relaxation as well as an intense focus. To help you practice these skills if you're a new to this activity Here are some suggestions:

1. Keep a consistent schedule: practice meditation at the same times each day. This will allow your mind move from the chaos and stress of the day to the calm and focused meditation more quickly because it operates in accordance with a regular biological clock. In the evening , before going to going to bed is an ideal time to sit in meditation because it can help you shed the negative energy that has built up throughout this day, and free your thoughts to prepare for meditation before you sleep.

2. Begin slowly: if have previously never meditated, begin with committing only 2 minutes a day to meditation. As your mind gets stronger, you'll be able to sit for longer durations of time, but beginning it is important not to meditate for long. Since, like physical exercise, if exert yourself too much, you'll end up feeling emotionally exhausted and stressed which is the complete opposite of what you're trying to accomplish through meditation.

3. Select your place: Choose an area that is quiet and relaxing where you can meditate every day. If it's a quiet garden bench or the tub in your home, choose the same spot every time.

4. Be at ease: you do not need to be in any particular way while meditation. The most important thing is to be relaxed. Do not wear clothing that can create discomfort or irritate and avoid sitting in a position that can cause tension or discomfort.

Dress in comfortable clothing, walk to your place and settle into a relaxed, comfortable place.

5. Be focused on your breath. The best way to cleanse your mind of the endless thoughts that are racing through it is to assign it a single task to concentrate on. Take a deep breath slowly and slowly, and feel how the air inhale fills your lungs, as it expands the chest. Be as focused as you can on every physical sensation you feel in your breath from exhalation to inhalation, and let all other thoughts within your mind go away every time you exhale.

There are many mantras that Buddhists utilize to concentrate their minds. There are 40 meditation topics that are commonly used. They are found in the classic Buddhist texts. Particularly, they can be located in the chapter 3 of Visuddhimagga.

Yoga

Yoga is yet another Buddhist method that has spread way beyond its original application in religion following its discovery to be a highly beneficial exercise for our health. Therefore, the concept is likely not completely new to you. If you've never practiced yoga before here are some helpful tips to get to the point of getting

1. Choose a yoga style There are a variety of types of yoga available which are most popular with beginners is hatha yoga or vinyasa yoga. The right type of yoga for you can help inspire you to continue practicing often.

2. Find an instructor: The most effective way to practice yoga is by having an instructor who is teaching the class. It is because classes follow the same schedule and help you stay on track and ensure that

you are practicing regularly. Additionally, you have the benefit of an experienced instructor who can assist you in improving your skills. The local gym or college might offer classes. If you aren't able to afford enough money to attend classes you can purchase an instruction video to practice yoga at your own home.

3. Make sure you have the proper apparatus: It's not that you require a lot of equipment to do yoga. The most important things are a yoga mat and comfortable (but appropriate) clothing. It is essential to have clothes that feel comfortable enough to practice the poses without the uncomfortableness from a tight waistband or stiff pants. Also, it is essential to make sure that your clothing is fitting. This doesn't mean you have to wear a tight, uncomfortable fit however, you shouldn't have the loose t-shirt to get

out of the way of performing the right pose.

The following tips will aid you in starting. Once you've started your journey, you'll soon get into a routine and figure the best method for you. The most important thing is to keep going. So, make sure you put in the proper determination!

Chapter 14: A New Way Of Seeing Yourself And The World

To discover what it's like to experience the world in a way that self-identification is decreased, try this exercise:

1. Take a seat and look around your surroundings, taking the time to soak everything in.

2. If you're ready to go to go, shut your eyes and let yourself relax.

3. Imagine you're an alien from another planet that has landed on Earth to investigate it. There is nothing you know about the planet or you have any prior experience to draw from. As a result, you're unable to categorize the meaning, recognize, analyze or evaluate anything you encounter. In the sense that you are completely blank.

4. Do not open your eyes and take a look around once more. Make sure to take your time.

5. What did your experience of observation compare to your initial observation?

If you didn't notice any distinction in the observations you made, try this exercise until you notice. When we integrate our thoughts or judgements when looking around, the thing being observed isn't being considered in a pure manner as our thoughts are projected on it. Being in a position to observe without the use of the concept of thinking is a an aspect of being aware and in the present.

Meditation

In the last exercise you will hopefully be able to experience at least for a moment the sensation to be free of mental thinking. The mind is a conceptual entity, and which is the way it functions. The mind transforms information we gather by using our five senses. If we receive information about the world around us via touch, perception hearing or hearing it is the mind that conceptualizes the information. The mind is not able to understand information that isn't extraordinary. Everything we experience is considered to be extraordinary, whereas everything that is not visible by our senses is deemed to be non-phenomenal. That's why we connect to our mind. Buddhism utilizes meditation to transcend mind to be able to see the mind's activities as well as live the world with greater clarity. This is a simple meditation that will assist you in creating space between yourself with your thoughts:

1. Find a peaceful spot to sit in that is comfortable. You can choose to sit on the floor or in a chair.

2. Put your eyes shut and let yourself ease into relaxation by focusing to the rhythm in your breathing. Focus on your breath when you breathe by focussing on the sensations you feel in your breath as you inhale. Repeat the same process when exhaling by focusing on the sensations you feel when your breath is released from your body.

3. Breathe normally as it is vital that you put in zero effort in this meditation.

4. A different method to observe breathing is to watch the rise and fall of your abdomen.

5. When you breathe, you'll feel thoughts, feelings of sensations, sounds, and thoughts and they'll have different features. Some may be enjoyable while others could be unpleasant or even scary. Whatever you experience don't interfere with them. Don't try to alter, control or

even analyze them. Be like scientists who are committed solely to watching them.

6. Be aware that everything you experience is temporary and indefinite. Your thoughts, perceptions and feelings will be revealed and disappear.

7. You are conscious of all these mental functions, however they aren't you. Your thoughts, perceptions or perceptions. You are not your feelings.

8. Concentrate your attention on an idea that you are currently experiencing. Be aware without judgement or trying to manage it. Watch the thought until it disappears. Are you able to identify the direction it took?

9. Focus your attention on an idea that appears within your mind. Are you able to identify the source of its arousal?

10. Then, track a thought in your attention until it is gone. When the next thought comes up What do you feel?

Your thoughts in the space could appear to be a blank, black space. Focus your focus on this space. When you are practicing this type of meditation, you'll be able increase the amount of time you spend in this area. This is a sign the fact that you've transcended the concept mind. You've gone beyond the realm of thought. This is the place that all mental phenomena come from. Through practice, you will be able to gain access to this space whenever you'd like. This is your gateway to Your Buddha nature.

Compassion

In Buddhism compassion is the ability to be aware of our connection to the whole universe. In the last meditation it was mentioned in the meditation that we are the place that all mental phenomena occur. These are then transferred to our lives. If you're on the beach, watching the beautiful sunset, how do you differentiate the experience of watching from the view of the sunset? What is the best way to distinguish the sound of the waves from the experience of listening? What can you do to separate the peace that you feel from the feeling? What can you do to separate your appreciation for the sunset from your thoughts? The most important part of your existence you are the only one who is aware of all mental processes. You are aware of sight and feeling sensations; your awareness is of thinking. Your awareness is distinct from mental phenomena, like the beach or the sun setting. Because you are aware and your own awareness, you are also inseparable from everything. Also, every aspect of existence is connected to consciousness. This means that all things are one. There is a component of yourself in everything you encounter. It is the most profound sense of compassion. It is to be capable of seeing yourself in everything.

Karma

Karma is one of the words that has gotten its place in the vocabulary of popular culture, however it is often overlooked. The word "karma" can be described as the Sanskrit word that means "action," and it comprises three parts that are memory, action, and desire. Let's consider the case of the food you love. When you first tried your favorite food, an entire sequence of events happened. The first one was desire, you had the desire to try the food. To enjoy your food you needed to act and reach to the food, and then try it. The experience of tasting food brought back memories of the event. The memory then triggered an urge to consume more of the food. Similar to food items that you don't like, the difference is that the memories of the food causes an urge to avoid that food in the near future. Karma is the regular behaviors and ways of thinking and the way of feeling that decide the direction in our daily lives. The issue is that actions are so deeply embedded within us that we're often not aware of it. It can become unconscious, leading us to think that our karma is what we are and is part of who we are.

The sole difference that exists between Bill Gates and a person who is living in poverty is their fate. In many religions and cultures the concept of karma is seen as being fixed, and that it is not able to be altered or that it requires several life-times to change, but this isn't the case. Your karma is created by you are the only one who is responsible for it. Let's look at the example of your most loved food. Each time you consume your favourite food, you've completed an karmic event. When you've eaten your food, it is clear that you have completed your karmic journey that has come to an end. Your karma will continue to be perpetuated when you next eat your favourite food. If you decide not to consume your favorite food in the future, you'd have ended this particular cycle of karmic karma.

Naturally, each of us is a victim to a variety of karma. It will take a lot of effort and time to stop our bad karma. That is the reason why taking up Buddhism can result in a huge change in your life. Instead of dealing with each incident of karma, Buddhism teaches how bring out your inner wisdom that will cause the negative karma you have to diminish their power. This is accomplished by bringing us to a higher degree of consciousness. This is the way to transform karma and awareness. The increased awareness you have is like that of the sun rising. The sun's light from the rising sun can cause the light of stars to diminish. The rising sun represents your ever growing awareness, and the stars represent your negative Karma.

Exercise

Karma is the way we have a habitual way of thinking and acting that have become embedded into our minds and behavior. Because of this, we are often unaware of our karma. If we do, it is often because we feel that there's nothing we can change it. The first step to changing our the karma of our lives is to be aware.

1. Be conscious of your day-to-day thoughts and actions.

2. If you are able to notice that you are thinking an idea that is a regular pattern or acting in a way that is habitual and you are not sure, ask yourself these questions:

1. Do I have the option of thinking differently or acting differently?

2. Does there have to be a remuneration in my thinking or interacting in this way?

3. How do I want to think in contrast to my current thinking patterns?

4. What would I prefer to behave in contrast to my usual behavior?

5. Are these new methods of thinking or behavior will yield the same benefits as my current way of thinking or behavior provides?

6. Do these methods of thinking or acting will bring me more happiness?

3. If you answered "yes" to both of the above questions, you can begin to incorporate your new ways of thinking or acting in your everyday life.

4. When you notice yourself repeating the same old thoughts or behaviour in a way that is not your own, remind yourself that you are now committed to the new ways of living.

Chapter 15: Breaking Down Buddhism

Once you've grasped a few of the basic ideas of Buddhism It's time to look at the more difficult questions in detail. With such a long experience and history, Buddhism has many complexities. This section is an opportunity to take your understanding to a whole new level.

What are the Four Noble Truths?

The Four Noble Truths are topics of thought. They aren't absolutes. Actually, there's only a few aspects of Buddhism which can be described as absolutes. Many consider nirvana to be the sole one.

The Four Noble Truths are ideals that are meant to be pondered over and contemplated with every encounter.

What is the First Noble Truth?

The first Noble truth is "Life is suffering". That implies that life is comprised of pain, disease as well as aging and death. The Buddhist name to describe suffering is "Dukkha." It embodies all kinds of suffering, which includes those experienced both emotionally and mentally. There is a lot of psychological pain: anger or embarrassment sadness, anger and isolation.

Dukkha is usually divided into three distinct types:

* Mental and physical pain dukkha-dukkha, also known as Dukkha-dukkha. The pain that comes to the cycles of existence: the aging process, birth, disease, and death.

* The hardship of change, referred to as Viparinamadukkha: a kind of suffering that comes with the anxiety and stress of changing and trying to keep the past.

* Unsatisfaction with life which is also known as Samkhara-dukkha. the normal unsatisfying feelings all living beings feel about their lives and the need to analyse and understand what is happening as well as the feeling that our expectations haven't been fulfilled.

It is common for us to experience suffering in our lives , in stark opposition to joy. Since Buddha was of the belief that pain could be overcome, and thus isn't a permanent thing, it could be concluded that He did not believe in the permanent nature of happiness. While he believed it was true but he also believed that it doesn't remain forever and that once it is gone the suffering will appear. Buddhists have been taught by their teachers to appreciate the relief from suffering that comes with the world. A lot of people achieve this by the pleasure of short-term pleasures However, the short-lived pleasures will never be able to overcome Dukkha.

The fact that suffering is inevitable cannot be disregarded. Human beings are not in control of the events that happen; they simply disappear of a person's life. This perspective is real and not too optimistic. Buddhism is a method of explaining how suffering can be prevented (or at the very least reduced) and ways to live a more peaceful and more satisfying life. If Buddha believed that suffering was an inexpressible fact one, then there'd be no way to overcome the issue in Buddhism.

This is crucial to anyone who interprets this to mean "everything is suffering." This is not true. Life's struggles are as significant as it is joy. Both concepts are fluid and are an integral part of living. The purpose for Buddhism is to achieve happiness that transcends all suffering, and as there could not be light without darkness, there is nothing but suffering.

What is the Second Noble Truth?

2. The second Noble Truth explains that the human suffering is due to aversion and desire. Humans will suffer for as long as believe that other people will be in agreement with us and to meet our expectations. Simply put, obtaining what you want doesn't ensure happiness.

The root reason for suffering, referred to as Samudaya is a reference to the ways we continue seeking external things to satisfy us. While we may be able to achieve our external goals and acquiring things of material value or doing other things that make us feel a little satisfied for a short time however, we will be disappointed and again at certain points. We will never be happy.

Second Noble Truth Second Noble Truth has three elements. These are the human desire for pleasure as well as the knowledge that desire must be released and the acceptance that desire is gone of. There are different names for the kinds of desire. Attachment and the cause of suffering originate from:

* The desire to feel enjoyment of the senses kama tanha

"The desire be Bhava Tanha

It is the desire rid yourself of vibhava Tanha

Buddha believed that the causes of cravings and thirst (tanha) result from lack of awareness of oneself. A thirsty and craving can cause mental and physical pain because it triggers the cycle of death and life. This is the notion of dependence that is arising from work. The consequence of the cause is suffering. The only way to end suffering is to end suffering.

Instead of battling to obtain what they want, individuals should alter their desire. The excessive desire for something deprives people of joy and satisfaction. An entire life of constant seeking and wanting (especially intense cravings such as ones for attention and immortality) produces a strong energy. This energy causes the person to reincarnate, as there is no way to be born again as someone who is able to comprehend the meaning of something without first wanting to understand what it actually means.

Reflection on this Second Noble Truth segues into the Third Noble Truth because it helps overcome the desires that result in suffering to lead to liberation.

What is the Third Noble Truth?

The third Noble Truth revolves around the ending of suffering. It states that one can conquer the suffering and pain of life and attain happiness. If we can let go of the useless desire and craving and live each day as an time, we can enjoy a happy and free life. It is important to let our desires fade and then to turn them off, give them up and let them go, both good and bad.

There are three phases to the third Noble Truth:

* The end of suffering.

• The recognition that the suffering must be a thing of the past

* And recognizing that you've finished your suffering

The goal of the third Noble Truth is to develop an awareness of the mind. Once you recognize that you are free of all illusions (suffering) then there's nothing that stands in the way of your journey to awakening. This truth can be a challenge for many , because it requires you to accept the non-suffering. You must separate yourself from your reactions and examine what you've in the past been attached to and the things you have been able to overcome.

It is important to realize what causes you to suffer, so that you don't endure any more suffering. Your soul will empty and the light of enlightenment will fill you. You'll be able to spend more time and energy and will be able to assist others, as your calmness and clarity will guide your steps.

What is the Fourth Noble Truth?

4. The fourth Noble Truth describes the Noble Eightfold Path as the final spiritual path to the ultimate end of suffering. You must be aware of the Path and believe in

the development of the Path and recognize that the Path is fully created to allow you to absorb the entirety in this truth.

What is the Noble Eightfold Path?

The Noble Eightfold Path is all about being morally aware of our words, thoughts and actions. We can develop wisdom by learning and comprehending The Four Noble Truths and developing compassion for others.

The Eightfold Path is often represented by an eight-spoked wheel. The spokes of this wheel represent those of the Four Noble Truths, Right Understanding and Right Aspiration. right speech, correct action Right Livelihood and Right Effort as well as Right Mindfulness and Right Concentration.

The various elements in the Eightfold Path are grouped together in the following sections:

1. Wisdom

A. Right Understanding

B. Right Aspriation

2. Morality

A. Right Livelihood

B. Right Speech

C. Right Action

3. Concentration

A. Right Effort

B. Right Concentration

c. Right Mindfulness

What is Dependent Arising?

Dependent arising, also known as Pratityasamutpada is a term that is portrayed throughout Buddhism. It is based on the notion that everything depends on other things, especially in how they come about or are created.

Based on their explanation of the manner that dukkha begins and is completed, based on the understanding of suffering's causes, and methods of overcoming the suffering The Four Noble Truths are considered to be the best illustration of the emergence of dependent.

Karma also arises dependently due to its dependence on the actions of others. In its simplest form, dependent arising is the basic principle of causality.

Depended Arising was the Buddha's own realization of Dharma. He experienced his own personal awakening and shattered desires within him. He was able to end his own suffering. The experience was so amazing that he decided he needed to share his path of thought with those who are looking to end themselves and let go of their burdens.

Dependent origination is composed of the 12 links that are dependent relationships that emerge. The links are as follows:

* Ignorance - Also known under the name "avijja," ignorance does not mean one is ignorant of anything at all. It's a way of saying that one is not completely aware the world around them. It is a state of mind that blocks oneself from all other beings and all phenomena. This is considered to be the cause of every evil. It's about not following the guidelines from The Four Noble Truths and the acknowledgment of dukka.

The result is an effect of fabrications

* Volitional and Fabrications The activities we engage in and the actions that we perform on other creatures can influence the results of these actions and behavior. What we do has the cause, and what happens afterwards is the consequence.

The result is an result of conditioned consciousness

* Conditioned consciousness: Thinking that we know the ways of things based on how our ears, eyes, tongues, noses and minds see. Making predictions based on prior experience or knowledge. It is necessary to renounce all prior information to have a second chance.

Effects of name and form

Name and form The notion that what's inside is what is influencing it externally. The sailor isn't an owner of the vessel Life can be the captain for the vessel. Minds and bodies have no claim on one another.

there are no owners. Name and form are interconnected but they are not one.

Effects from the sense base sixfold

* Six-fold sense bases , which are the functions of our ears, tongue, nose and our minds. The gateways through which we acquire our impressions as well as interact with others or other entities.

The result is the result of contact

* Contact - the times when things, senses or organs are brought into consciousness, causing people to differentiate between something that is bad, good or neutral. It distinguishes between the encounter with an object and then labeling an object, studying it or processing it into its own.

This results in the feeling of sensation

* Feeling is the part of your brain that is able to experience the positive, negative and neutrality in contact. When data is

able to reach desire, and it is able to perceive feelings. Feelings generate desire. The pleasure of feeling creates an urge to seek more, whereas negative feelings trigger the desire to stay away from. It is good to be happy, however, hurt causes suffering, and impartial judgments are often discarded without notifying.

This can cause the sensation of craving

* Craving is a level of desire. The psychological factor that indicates desire , but is not related to satisfaction. There are six types of cravingthat are related to sounds, forms and smells, tastes, the touch and thoughts. Every form evokes thirst.

This can be a result of grasping

* Grappling (clinging) A degree of desire greater than the desire. It is broken down into view attachment as well as self attachment as well as practice attachment

and sexual attachment. It's a state of mind which clings to an object and imprisons the mind.

The result is of being

* Becoming is the time between the full potentialization of a person and the Reincarnation. The moment when your life's current one has been praised and you are awaiting the rebirth into a new one. The broken down of forms becoming sensual, being a form, and then non-formless becoming

The result is the feeling of Rebirth

* Rebirth is the attainment in a different status regardless of form, mentality or place. The process of becoming anew by physical form, emotion or awareness.

o Resulting in death

* Death is a certain state of obscurity in which ignorance and ignorance are the norm.

Many think that twelve link explains the cause of suffering. They Buddhists make use of the links to justify their own to deny self. Others Buddhists consider that they confirm the non-existence of our existence via the concept of relativity. Some still interpret them as a reason for emptyness. Since all the links are contingent and dependent they aren't independently real and are not able to stand on their own as reality of our being. However, since we all take part in the interdependence of everything that we are not real and empty.

If you don't understand the concept of Dependent Arising, you're at the source of all pain. This is among the most crucial links in Buddhism. It is present in numerous of its teachings and is a valid argument for the path each Buddhist has to take to attain an enlightenment. The ability to comprehend the teachings of Dependent Arising can't be denied - regardless of the number of books studied or thought processes are examined. You have to be a part of the process in your own personal life and discover the lessons it teaches your body and mind.

What is Karma?

The law that governs Karma is cause and result. That is, every action is a consequence. This simple law can be explained as follows:

What is the reason for the lack of equality all over the world?

* Why do some people seem handicapped , while other people are talented?

* Why do certain people only live for a short period of time?

What is the best way to determine the karmic consequences and effects that their choices have on them? Think about the following:

* The motivation behind the act

* The effects and repercussions of this action on oneself

* The consequences and effects of this action on other people

Although many view karma as an unrelated notion, it has roots that go back further that Buddhism itself. Karma has a long and rich history within Indian culture, and it is only natural that it is mentioned in Buddhist doctrines.

The differences between different humans require an explanation. If you look at those who are blind, deaf or disabled it's easy to ask what caused their unfortunate fate to them and not to you. Certain

Buddhists might consider karma to be the solution.

It's a controversial subject. You don't want to blame someone else for the circumstances that led to their suffering However, in the Buddhist world it is believed that what happens around goes around. If you suffer from extreme suffering this is typically viewed as an effect of your thinking and actions in your previous life. This is the most likely explanation.

The inequality of life does not have anything to do with nature or. nature or genes. It's all about Karma which is our past as well as our present. Since we are accountable for our actions how we behave when being reincarnated is an exact mirror of how we conducted our previous lives.

Buddha acknowledged that we have characteristics in our lineage. However, he did not allow this idea to undermine the notion that no matter the place or person we come from, we all have the power to defeat the inherent power inside our own souls. The cumulative karma of a lifetime can outweigh many genetic conditions. Consider, for example, that of the Buddha himself.

Buddha was born from 2 normal fathers. Their egg and sperm along with their genes and their lifestyle made him. However, despite having a lot in common with his parents , or other family members He was still more significant than the others. He was able to learn more, share more knowledge and appreciate life better than anyone else. This could have been his amazing Karma.

What are the Five Precepts?

The main moral codes in Buddhism include the five Precepts:

Never take the life of a living thing which includes all living creatures. The right of living beings to live and respecting their right.

* Never accept anything you don't want to be provided. It is applied within a sense of. If you're not certain that it is intended for you, don't do it.

Beware of sexual harassment and don't overindulge in sexual pleasures. It refers to excessive indulgence of any kind. This includes sexual and gluttony.

* Avoid false or misleading speech. It is applicable to any speech. Incapsulates deceit, lies, and slander too.

Beware of intoxication to maintain your focus. It does not impose a necessary evil to substances. Instead, it talks about being careful about indulgences, since it may result in breaking the earlier rules.

Mahayana Buddhists usually adhere to strict vegetarianism as they believe it is the best understanding of the First Precept. They believe that eating animals is an act of taking the animal's life.

What is the best way to choose from Theraveda, Mahayana and Vajrayana Buddhism?

Buddhism has many paths individuals can take to attain the state of enlightenment. Theraveda offers the opportunity for people to follow "The Way of the Elders" and attain the personal path to enlightenment. This is only possible by achieving nirvana. Nirvana is the feeling of happiness and knowledge which transcends pain. Theraveda Buddhists typically become monks and focus on their own Nirvana.

Theraveda Buddhism is popular in the southern part of Asia. The first teachings of this religion can be found in Pali writings and is described as being quite conventional. Theraveda Buddhists are able to acknowledge that Buddha was human and that he had the ability to comprehend human mental nature with a strong concentration on meditation and the transformation of the individual's consciousness. They believe Buddha is adamant that his followers to avoid evil, to accumulate goodness and cleanse their minds. These objectives can be achieved through the three trainings including meditation, insight-wisdom and the formation of ethical behavior.

Theraveda Buddhists are of the belief that all things around the globe has the same three traits. First, they aren't forever and are not permanent. They also have a transiency. Furthermore, all phenomena in the world have nothing that can be considered one's own, which can lead to discontent. Finally, the Theravedan Buddhists think that all compounds contain two components, one of the non-material as well as that made up of material. The compounded objects contain five distinct groups. The first is their physical quality. The remaining four are not material which include feelings and perception, mental formatives and consciousness.

Mahayana Buddhists put off their own nirvana for the sake of helping others. They place humanity before their own and assist others to find the way towards the path to salvation.

Mahayana was developed through members of the Mahasanghikas sect, a earliest section that was a part of Buddhist seceders. Their specific form of Buddhism was quickly gaining popularity because of the changes that they made in the conventional guidelines of Buddhism. They changed a number of rules for monastics that directly affected those who were part of the Buddhist Order of Monks. They also proposed various arrangements that incorporated their Sutra along with the Vinaya The texts contain the original texts and the rules.

Mahayana The Buddhists of Mahayana believe they're linked externally to the world and all the life it carries. Within this particular sect there are two different systems of thought. Madhyamikas are a strong advocate of an intermediate path. They don't believe in the existence of God or non-reality or the reality of this world. Instead, this group is focused on the concept of relativity and takes Buddhist's ethical understanding on the Middle path and places it into the metaphysical.

The other Mahayana group of Buddhists is called the Yogacara. The Yogacara emphasize the practice of yoga and meditation in order to reach their absolute spiritual truth. They believe there are ten levels of spiritual growth that Buddhists must complete before they are able to attain Bodhi.

Vajrayana Buddhistism also referred to by its other name, Tantric Buddhism, was developed in India and Tibet. It is different from Mahayana Buddhism in practice however, it does not differ in philosophy. Another name for this type in Buddhism is Mantrayana. The term is used to describe the use of mantras to stop Vajrayana Buddhism from departing from their goal and purpose. Because it is concerned with personal experiences, Vajrayana uses an extremely symbolic language to help followers identify their own inner experiences. In the end, these are the experiences that are thought to be to be the most valuable and most in line with the experiences of Buddha.

Vajrayana Buddhism requires a certain amount of mystical experiences in order to achieve bliss. It is the third major Yana (vehicle) of Buddhism Vajrayana is the type of Buddhism that is associated with Lamas and Gurus. The practitioners must be introduced to this particular form of Buddhism through gurus or spiritual guides.

What is the story behind how the three different varieties of Buddhism come about?

There is a belief that there were three turns of the Dharma wheel. The first turn resulted in The Four Noble Truths. These Four Noble Truths lead into the Hinayana schools among in which Theravada

Buddhism has been the sole remaining sect.

The second revolution of the wheel produced the fruits of the Perfection of Wisdom sutras, which started with the Mahayana schools.

The third turn of the wheel was centered on all beings with the Buddha-nature. This turn led for the Vajrayana and the realization of the absolute truth through tantric practices.

The Timeline of Buddhism

The rich and varied history of Buddhism is filled with events that took place many thousands many years back. These events remain relevant to today's Buddhists and are significant in bringing about shifts in Buddhist the past. Since Buddhism is different from country nation, it's simpler to follow its development by looking at changes within one country at an time.

When you go through the timeline, you'll observe that it begins to provide details about every country as Buddhism changed and evolved into something bigger.

Check out this extensive chronology of Buddhism and get absorbed in the ways that it has developed. Be aware that the years are dated by BCE (before common time) in addition to CE, Common Era.

The Buddha's Lifetime (BCE)

*563: Siddharth Gautama is born to an aristocratic Nepalese clan in Lumbini

* 534. Gautama abandons the royal title and wealth behind to seek wisdom, initially through the process of hunger.

*528: In the Bodhi tree, the Buddha is able to attain enlightenment in Bodh Gaya India. He is transferred to a town named Sarnath to deliver his first sermon, focused on the Dharma. The Dharma concept transforms lives.

* 483 * 483 Buddha dies in Kushinagar within India.

The Buddhist Councils (BCE)

* 483 3 months after The first Buddhist council meets.

*400s The Gandhari script becomes popular. The script was written using an old script that gave crucial insight to the first council.

*383: The 2nd Buddhist council is held at Vaishali, India.

* 367 * 367: A non-canonical Buddhist council is held in Pataliputra.

*300. The year of the oldest Brahmi script ever to have been found

* 250 The King Ashoka needs his third Buddhist meeting to take place. This is also

the time of the beginning of the full Kharosthu script.

1. 1st Century CE 4. Buddhist council is held at India under the leadership of Kanishka.

The Dispersion of Buddhism (BCE)

220: The king Ashoka sends an official in Sri Lanka. Mahinda, the missionary Mahinda introduced Theravada Buddhism to the Sri Lankan people, including the King Devanampiya Tissa.

*180: India is taken by Demetrius, an emperor of Greco-Bactrian origins. Demetrius travels all up to Pataliputra and establishes what would become known as"Indiana," or the Indo-Greek Kingdom. Buddhism grows in both popularity and size under Demetrius the emperor.

*150: Meander, a king of Demetrius The Indo-Grecian kingdom begins to study

Buddhism under the direction of a sage Guru known as Nagasena (Milinda Panha).

*120 The Chinese Emperor called Han Wudi accepts the gift of two Buddha statues in gold. At Dunhuang City, Records of these transactions were discovered within the Mogao caves.

*29: The first Pali cannon is documented by the people of Sri Lanka, the home of Theravada.

Common Era Buddhism

* 1st Century

The practice of Buddhism is recognized as a valid religion Buddhism becomes relevant in China. The first method in Buddhism within China is documented. The monks Chufarlan and Moton introduce it to the country. The following season, China is awed by the construction of the White Horse temple and recognizes

Buddhism as a faith system. Buddhism begins to decline around the year 78 CE when the power of a Chinese general takes over the power of a Buddhist nation.

* 2nd Century

in 116 CE: Kanishka takes over numerous Buddhist nations and becomes the ruler of. In the past, these nations relied on the Chinese and under his reign they become Kushaka. In the years following the monk and the prince would begin translating Buddhist text into Chinese for better understanding and distribution to the general public. He picks to translate the Mahayana books and becomes known for being the very first Chinese translator.

It is when Buddhists start to show interest in Vietnam and begin to travel there to find out more about the country's people and its land

* 3rd Century

296 CE. first date ever recorded in any Chinese document of Buddhism

* 4th Century

O Koreans acknowledge Buddhism as a faith system and the religion begins to become popular.

O Fa- Hien travels to India from his home in China. He learns from his experiences and translate the same between 399 and 414 CE.

It is Nalanda University in India grows ever more renowned. It's a well-known an educational centre for Buddhists and is home to 10,000 students.

* 5th Century

o Sri Lankan philosopher Buddhaghosa become popular. He oversees the erection of the stupa at Dambulla the Funan kingdom in Cambodia is a testament to the appeal and rationality of Buddhism that makes it appealing to many.

Scientists have attributed to the Pali writings to be from the time of this. These documents are essential to Buddhist time and culture.

Kumarajiva is brought to China in the capacity of translator, and starts translating Buddhist texts into Chinese. Shortly after, Hui Yuan decrees that it is Buddhist monks don't have to bow before the Chinese Emperor. In the year 405 CE Kumarajiva is recognized with a visit from Yao Xing, who requested his visit. In 405 CE, Buddhabhadra arrives in China and begins preaching Buddhism to a large number of people. In memory of and gratitude to his wisdom The Shaolin Temple is built in his honour.

It is believed that Buddhism is located in Sumatra. It is the first known period for Buddhism throughout Indonesia.

* 6th Century

The great Bodhidharma arrived in China in the year 520 CE. He is from India and is able to settle in the monastery. After 60 years, a brand new dynasty comes to China. Buddhism gains popularity. This is often referred to as Buddhism's"Golden" Age throughout China.

O Vietnam is witnessing the emergence to Zen Buddhism. Kind Khosrau is demanding that tales from Jataka include Persian translations.

538 C.E. Japan introduces Buddhism and adopts it in a wildly. Buddhism is the main national religion by the time this century comes to an end. Many experts think that Buddhism was introduced 14 years later rather than.

* 7th Century

The sutras are made of tone found in Fangshan, Yuzhou - sometime about the beginning of the 600s.

A. The Chinese Tang dynasty rises to the heights of power in the monarchy of China

O Tibet introduces Buddhism.

* 8th Century

O Jataka stories are translated to Arabic as well as Syrian in a number of cities.

It is the time when the Japanese Nara period in the history of Japan starts and flourishes. Chinese monk Jianzhen arrives in Japan and begins to build Japanese Ritsu School. Japanese Ritsu School.

the first Tibetan monastery is built and is constructed along with the initial School of Tibetan Buddhism, known as Samye and the Nying-mapa school and Nying-ma-pa school, respectively.

* 9th Century

o Monks establish Japanese Buddhist schools in 804 CE. These schools are known as "the Japanese Shingon School and the Japanese Tendai School

O Buddhist are targeted and exiled across China

O Buddhism declines in Tibet as a result of fear and confusion

* 10th century

O Buddhism is seen to return within Tibet with a large tradition that is backed by a strong

O The Buddhist temple of Bagan is built by the Buddhists of Myanmar, Burma.

In 983, the publishing of Chinese Buddhist texts is complete. This is during the period during the Song dynasty.

A replica of this cannon was received from Korea.

* 11th century

It is believed that the Sakya-pa School of Tibetan Buddhism has been established. Numerous monks from all over Asia visit to study there.

The Korean monks carve woodblocks of Buddhist texts to print

It is believed that the Theravada School of Buddhism returns in Sri Lanka. Burma is joined by Sri Lankans to adopt Buddhism and also

o At the same time in the birthplace of Buddhism, India, popularity is decreasing

* 12th century

The emperor Dao becomes the leader Dao is elected as the leader. Buddhism begins to decline. Dao will make a conscious effort to discredit the religion

The Cambodian Buddhism Jayavarman VII constructs Bayon Temple as part of Angkor Temple Complex. The complex was the home of numerous Theravada people who converted to Buddhism in the future.

O Pure Land School of Buddhism was established in Japan alongside The Rinzai Zen School of Japanese Buddhism.

O Burmese Buddhism becomes it's own sect following a transition from Sri Lankan Theravada

The center for learning, Nalanda University is overtaken and was sacked

* 13th century.

o the founder of Nichiren Buddhism, Nichiren Daishonin was originally from

Japan. Japan also has it's Caodong School of Zen. This monk also teaches Dogen Zenji, Eiheiji Soto Zen Temple and Monastary are also in existence.

O Theravada Buddhism is now the official religion in Thailand. It is more popular than Mahayana in popularity and is a favorite among the Thai.

The Mongols have taken over their place in the Theravada Kingdom to Pagan.

O Theravada Buddhism gains popularity in Mahayana Buddhism in Cambodia and Sri Lanka

* 14th Century

Ayutthaya was named the capital city of Thailand

Bu-ston edits and compiles Tibetan Buddhist canons. First Dalai Lama is born in Tibet

* 16th century

for the very first time in the history of humankind, Altan Khan gives Sonam Gyatso an official title. He is now the 3rd Dalai Lama.

* 17th century

The practice of Japanese Buddhism is controlled by a dictatorship known as The Tokugawa Shogunate. There is a strong resemblance to Buddha was created in a temple of Toyotomi family. Toyotomi family.

Divided Vietnam has two distinct varieties of Buddhism.

O Mongols accept Gelug-pa Buddhism in Tibet. In the Khan of Khoshuud bestows the fifth Dalai Lama with the right to rule of Tibet.

* 18th century

Ayutthaya is targeted and several Buddhist wisdoms don't pass through the seizure of paper.

* 19th century

The Monkhood has been modified in Thailand. The changes are practiced today by many knowledgeable monks

The Buddhists of Shanghai created in Shanghai the Jade Buddha temple complete with the Jade Buddha statue brought from Burma.

The practice of Buddhism is a religion that has some limitations within Vietnam under Nguyen Anh , and the following Minh Mang for nearly 40 years

An Sri Lankan revival of Buddhism grows in popularity. The Buddhist belief system spreads like wildfire. This revival comes at a crucial juncture and will help spread

Buddhism across Asia for many years to follow.

O Buddhism is introduced to Chicago in 1893 when two monks travel for the World Parliament of Religions in Chicago in 1893.

First time ever in the past 100 years this is the first time that the Buddhist Council meets. Fifth Buddhist council met at the end of 1871 in Mandalay. Stones that commemorate the Pali cannon was engraved in honor of the King of Burma and placed around the monastery which hosted the council. The moment the British were in control of Burma, Gordon Douglas becomes the first Western Theravada Buddhism to have an official ordination in Burma.

A stone representation of King Ashoka was discovered in Nepal in 1896.

* 20th century

The first Buddhist temple is discovered at the United States in 1922. It was founded by the Zen Studies Society of New York is a support mechanism for D.T. Suzuki. The universities and learning centers across the country start to open with the encouragement of Buddhism. There are societies and institutes across the entire coast including California as well as the Northeastern seaboard.

The Chinese caves near the top of a popular Buddhist travel destination are open to be examined once more.

The Communists of Laos request that monks be involved in a way to better influence citizens. This is among the biggest flaws in Buddhism in Laos since it has led monks to return to the common life, as well as hindered the growth and understanding of Buddhism as an approach to living.

O Buddhism in India changes and expands. New temples are built , and followers are added to the thousands. A Buddhist nun's organization is relaunched in Sarnath.

O Cambodia is a victim of persecution of Buddhism. Monks are killed or taken out to different countries to dismantle the belief system. Nearly all Cambodian Buddhist temple is put to ruin.

The situation in Tibet: Chinese forces occupy Tibet and force the 14th Dalai Lama and his followers to leave for India. Buddhist monastery located in Tibet have been destroyed, and Buddhist practitioners are punished.

the World Fellowship of Buddhists is founded within Colombo, Sri Lanka. It is the World Buddhist Council allies with the World Fellowship of Buddhists and assists when necessary however even this strong alliance cannot stop certain Sri Lankan

Buddhist temples from being destroyed and terrorized.

the Burmese security forces continue to abuse and oppress Buddhist monks throughout Burma. It is extremely difficult for Buddhist monks to the time to practice their faith since their suffering is intensified

The Borobodur Borobodur is being restored in Indonesia thanks to the efforts by the Indonesian Archaeological Service and UNESCO.

* 21st century

There are a number of training and sanitation facilities are now open in Malaysia

Two temples have been dismantled to be destroyed by Taliban within Afghanistan. The monuments are dedicated to Buddhism and its principles.

Chapter 16: The Circumstances For The Potentials For Happiness To Ripen

The way we experience thoughts or objects - either in terms of happiness or sadness is not determined, it is determined by the item or thoughts themselves. We have observed that, if through our long-term past behavior, we've established the habit of not overstating or denial of their positive and negative sides of thoughts or objects it is possible to feel the suffering of having to undergo root canal treatment with a relaxed mindset. In the context of the definition that happiness is a state of mind, then we go through the process in a pleasant way, with the belief that it will be beneficial for ourselves.

While we may have developed a habit of not or speaking when we are afflicted by disturbing emotions and have thus built up the possibility of experiencing objects and thoughts that are happy However, certain conditions are essential for this possibility to develop into a feeling of happiness. We've learned that the object that we experience doesn't necessarily dictate the degree to which we experience it with happiness or discontent. Instead, the perception of objects with joy is more dependent on our mindset of accepting the real-world fact of what the object is regardless of what the object may be, such as the physical pain of root canal treatment or the appearance of an individual we love. Our attitude and mental state is crucial to determine whether we are feeling happy or miserable regardless of the object we may be looking at or hearing, smell and tasting, sensing physically or thinking about.

We've also noticed that when we acknowledge the truth of what we see and do not get too naive about it, we don't exaggerate or dismiss its positive or bad aspects, so we don't experience the object in lust or greed or in anger or repulsion. So, what can bring about the growth of happiness at any given moment is letting go of ignorance.

Naivety

In any particular time of unhappy the naivety of our minds isn't always limited to being naive regarding the thing we're facing. Naivety has a wider scope. It is also a focus on us. If we're experiencing problems that cause us to be unhappy or sadness, we can become focused solely on ourselves. We may think it is the sole ones who has ever had this issue.

Consider the scenario loss of our employment. There is a lot of individuals across the globe who had their job taken away and are without a job. We can consider our current situation, but not be naive regarding the impermanence of things, for example. We should remember that every phenomenon that result from causes and situations are influenced by other factors and conditions and will ultimately be over. It can be very beneficial. However, it is even more efficient expanding the thought process to include not just our own, but also the other employees' concerns of losing their job, if they have experienced this. We must consider "This isn't solely my problem and it's the problem of an overwhelming amount of people. It is not just me that is the only one in need of an answer. Everyone else requires a solution, too. Everyone must overcome these difficulties and discontent." This is in fact the situation.

This way of thinking, that is unbiased it is possible to develop empathy towards others instead of being self-absorbed and pityful. Our minds aren't solely focused on us and are more flexible in considering the other people in a similar situation. In order to assist those in need to overcome their challenges also, our own personal issues become less important and we gain the confidence and determination to face these issues in a non-biased way. We certainly didn't want to be fired from our position however, we are able to accept the fact of the matter and, when we consider the situation of others perhaps we are satisfied that we are now given the chance to help others.

The relationship between compassion and Happiness

The concept of compassion is one of the primary factors that can trigger our ability to see something or someone with joy.

How does it work? The concept of compassion is that we want people to be free from their suffering as well as the reasons for their pain in the same way that we wish that for us. When we are focused on the pain and the unhappiness of other people, we tend to find ourselves feeling sad and not content. We may also block emotions and not feel anything. In any event we're not content with their situation. How can compassion help bring happiness to a mental state?

To comprehend this, we must distinguish the upsetting (zang-zing) emotions in contrast to other (zang-zing med-pa) emotions. In this case, I'm using these terms without their precise definitions however in a more informal non-technical sense. The distinction is how much the feeling of happiness, sadness or neutral is mingled with uncertainty and naivety about the emotion itself. Remember, when we distinguished happiness from unhappy generally, the primary factor was the degree to which we were ignorant about the situation that we felt. Even when we don't make up or denigrate the attributes of an object we feel unhappy about such as, for instance it is possible to make the unhappy feeling into some kind of real, existing "thing," like a deep dark cloud that is hanging on our shoulders. Then, we exaggerate the negative characteristics of the sensation and make it appear to be, for example, "a horrible depression" and feel trapped within the feeling. In this scenario, lack of a sense of reality is not accepted as the feeling of sadness for the fact that it is. In the end, the feeling of sadness is something that is constantly changing in a moment-to-moment manner depending on its intensity. it's not a kind of solid object that exists on its on its own, without any influence from any other factors.

The same approach to not feeling anything at all when we think about the suffering of other people. If we magnify the negative qualities of feeling unhappy or sad and are afraid to feel it, and we shut it out. In the end, we feel an uninvolved feeling, not satisfied or happy. We then exaggerate that neutral feeling by imagining that it is something solid, such as the big strong "nothing" that is sitting in us, and is hindering us from truly experiencing something.

To cultivate compassion, it's important not to overlook the tough situations of others can be sad, just as they are ours, like we lose our job. It is not healthy to avoid feeling this sadness, or block or deny it. It is important to experience this sadness with a gentle manner so that we can be able to feel the suffering of others and to cultivate the sincere desire for others to be free from it and accept some responsibility to assist them in overcoming it. In simple terms it is that the Buddhist guidance is "Don't make a solid 'thing' out of feeling sad; don't make a big deal out of it."

Quieting the Mind

To experience the feelings of sorrow in a peaceful way, we must clear our minds of any thoughts of dullness and mental wandering. If we wander our minds drift off to disturbing thoughts like thoughts that are filled with anxiety and fear, doubt or thoughts full of expectations of what we believe to be a more enjoyable experience. When we are dull it is easy to get lost in a fog of thoughts and lose our focus on all things.

Buddhism is a rich source of methods to rid our mind of wandering thoughts and dullness. A fundamental techniques is to relax by focusing our attention on breathing. With no mental turbulence and mental fatigue our minds become calm and calm. When we are in a calm state, we are able to more easily relax, as well as any exaggeration , repulsion or indifference to other people's troubles and suffering, as well as the feelings we have about them. If we do initially find ourselves feeling sad, it's not causing us to feel upset.

In the end, as our minds settles down , we naturally experience a lower level of happiness. When we are in a calm psychological and mental state the inherent warmth and joy of the mind apparent. If we've developed the necessary potential for experiencing satisfaction through constructive behaviour, our calm state of mind can allow them to mature and grow.

Developing Love

Then we enhance our happiness by thinking about love. The definition of love is that it is the desire that others are content and have the motivations to be happy. The desire for happiness naturally comes from a compassionate understanding. Although we may feel sad about an individual's sorrow and pain and sadness, it can be difficult when we are actively trying to wish that person be happy. If we put aside thoughts about ourselves and concentrate instead on the happiness of another person our hearts naturally warm. This instantly brings us another sense of happiness, and could bring about more possibilities to be happy, which were constructed over time due to our positive actions. So, when you are truly loving and sincere it is accompanied by a peaceful happiness it, which isn't upsetting and sadness is wiped away. As parents suffering from headaches forgets about the pain by comforting the child who is sick and the sorrow that we feel when someone's luck isn't ours is gone when we are surrounded by thoughts of the love of our lives.

Chapter 17: How To Meditate

If you are reading books on contemplation, or more often when contemplation is displayed in various settings there is a significant portion of the emphasis is placed on the techniques. In the West people tend to be highly influenced to what they consider to be the "innovation" of contemplation. However the truth is that the most crucial aspect of contemplation is not the method however, it is the process to be the soul. This is called"the "stance", a stance that is not at all physical, but more about your soul or the mental state.

It is important to realize that when you embark on an exercise in contemplation it is an extremely surprising dimension of reality. In our lives, we typically invest a lot of effort to accomplishing tasks that require an immense amount of struggle involved in contemplation, but it is the opposite and is a departure from the routine work we do.

It is an issue of becoming melting, like the spread that is left out in the sun. It is nothing to do with of whether or not you "know" anything about it in reality when you practice the process of contemplation, it should be clear, as if you were doing the first time. Simply sit down in a quiet place, your body still with your thoughts quiet and your brain is calm and let thoughts flow around and around, not giving them a chance cause havoc on your mind. In the event that you need to take a break take a look at the soothing. This is a simple procedure. When you breathe out, you must realize that you're breathing out. When you breathe in, you must realize that you're taking in without offering any type of further review or disguised mental conversation and only focusing on your breath. The simple act of treatment focuses your thoughts and emotions, and then as if you were shedding the shed of old skin and discarded, something gets removed and released.

The majority of people have a tendency to unwind their body through focussing on different areas. Unwinding is truly when you release the body from within and everything else will be dialed out in a normal manner.

When you begin to practice the technique, you concentrate yourself on the area of "weakness", and simply keep it there. You don't have to be focused on any specific thing at all. Just be open let your thoughts and emotions to relax. If you choose to do this and then afterward, when you employ an approach, such as taking a breath in and focusing on the breath, your focus will be more naturally focus on relaxation. There isn't a specific spot in the breath that you need to focus your attention and it's basically an approach to relaxation. 25 percent of your attention is focused on your breath and 75% of it is just informal. Try to connect with the breath, rather than just taking note of it. You can choose a symbol like a flower like a rose or a flower to focus on. Sometimes, you are asked to imagine an illumination on the temple or inside the heart. Every now and then, the sound of a mantra or a sound could be used. Whatever you choose, at the beginning it is best to remain open, like the sky. Imagine yourself as the sky, which holds the entire universe.

Sitting down, allow things calm and allow your self-defying doubts and unnaturality to disappear and rise to reveal your true self. You discover a portion of you that is genuine and more authentically and the "genuine" you. As you move on you discover and interact with your fundamental goodness.

The purpose of reflection is to adjust to a perspective you've missed. The word "reflection" in Tibetan "reflection" signifies "getting used to".

Now , you might ask How do you get used to it? You need to be able to accept your true nature that is that is your Buddha nature. This is why you get the most amazing educating of Buddhism and Dzogchen In it, you are instructed to "rest in the way of psyche". It is a simple process of sitting and let your thoughts and thoughts disintegrate. It's similar to when the mists dissolve or the fog disperses and you can see the distinctive skies and sun shining down. If everything breaks down in this manner, you begin to discover your true nature, and begin to "live". The moment you realize itand, right there and there, you're feeling better than normal. It's not as similar to other feelings of happiness that you've experienced. This is real and genuine goodness where you experience an overwhelming sense of peace as well as satisfaction and confidence about your self.

How to Begin Meditating

Correctly preparing yourself

To focus on our thinking, we require a comfortable seat and a solid posture. The most important aspect of a good posture is to keep the back straight. In order to accomplish this, if you are sitting on a pad, we make sure your pad's back is slightly more elevated than its front, and slanting our pelvis a bit towards the front. It may seem a bit overwhelming initially to be seated with legs folded however it's an ideal idea to be able to transition to the posture that is the stance of Buddha Vairochana. In the event that we aren't able to maintain this stance, we should sit in the same position as the same as is possible and still be comfortable.

The seven main components of Vairochana's position are:

Legs are cross-legged in the vajra position. This reduces the musings and feelings of envy.

* The right hand is placed on the left side, with palms up with the fingers' tips marginally raised and gently touching. Hands are held approximately four fingers' length below the navel. This allows us to develop focused. The right hand is a symbol of technique while the left hand is a symbol of ability to make decisions - both represent the fusion of intelligence and strategy. The two thumbs that are at the navel level symbolise the burst of the internal fire.

It is straight in the back, but not in a tense state. This allows us to develop and maintain a decent persona, and allows the natural vitality to flow freely.

* The teeth and lips are secured but the tongue is pressed against the top of the teeth. This reduces the amount of saliva we produce while also preventing our mouths from becoming dry.

The head is tilted slightly forward, with the jaw slightly folded in such that the eyes are turned downwards. This stops the mental excitement.

The eyes are not fully closed or open however they are half-open and look downwards along the nasal line. If eyes are fully open, we'll probably be able generate mental energy, and when the eyes are closed, we're likely to experience mental sinking.

The shoulders are at a level while the elbows have been kept apart from the sides in order so that air has a chance to flow.

When we sit down to reflect, our mind is typically awash with unpleasant thoughts but we're not able to immediately transform this view into the moral one we want to use to inspire us. A negative, exasperates perspective resembles pitch-dark fabric. We aren't able to color pitch-dark fabric or any other shade except that we first eliminate all the dark hue and then make the fabric white again. Also, in the event that we want to paint our brains with a sensible inspiration, it is necessary to collect all of our negative thoughts and diverting thoughts. It is possible to achieve this through breathing meditation.

Breathing properly

After we've settled effortlessly in our contemplation stance it is time to be aware of the thoughts and divergences that are forming within our minds. Then we gently shift our attention to our breath, allowing its breath a chance to remain regular. When we exhale, we imagine that we are inhaling endlessly, all the exasperating thoughts and distractions in a dark cloud disappears into space. When we breathe in, our breath, we can imagine being absorbed by all the blessings and motives of the stars as white light that penetrates our bodies and stays in our hearts.

We continue to experience this sensation each and every breath and exhalation for 21 cycles or until our psyche has been revealed to be calm and cautious. If we concentrate on our actions in this direction, any distractions and negative thoughts are likely to disappear in light due to the fact it is impossible to concentrate upon more than one issue at any time. When we have finished our breath-based meditation, we should to reflect on 'Now I've received the blessings and inspiration of all the holy creatures.' Our brain appears to be a pure white fabric that we are able to now shade with an upright source of inspiration such as empathy or the bodhichitta.

In the next chapter I'll share a technique for meditation for those who are new to meditation.

Conclusion

We've seen, through during the span of this publication, how important the doctrines from Buddha. We have also seen the importance of his teachings by Buddha and what the specific teachings are so that we can incorporate them into our daily lives as we strive to change them to be more effective.

We've also witnessed the most effective ways to implement these lessons into our lives in just seven days. If you begin on Monday, for instance you don't need to wait until the following Sunday to see if you've absorbed these concepts to the maximum of your abilities. It is because they are fundamental principles that everyone can implement to alter our lives to the best of our abilities.

In time, you'll begin to experience your life changing in a way that is enchanting. In the initial few days, you will notice a positive change in your life. This will inspire you to push further towards completing the path that the Buddha has laid so beautifully out for us all.

It's the right time to get started to walk the spiritual path to ensure that you can inject your life with the most positive energy you've ever dreamed of!

www.ingramcontent.com/pod-product-compliance
Lightning Source LLC
Chambersburg PA
CBHW071824080526
44589CB00012B/909